COCKS ONLY

PIFFA SCHRODER

with illustrations by
TIMOTHY JAQUES

SWAN·HILL
PRESS

By the same author and published by Gun Room Publishing:
Fair Game. Banging On. Bird's Eye View. Bags & Baggage.

First published in the UK 2003
by Swan Hill Press, an imprint of Quiller Publishing Ltd

Illustrations copyright © Timothy Jaques, 2003

British Library Cataloguing-in-Publication Data

A catalogue record for this book is available from The British Library

ISBN 1 904057 33 0

Cover illustration and design by Timothy Jaques

Typeset by: Mel-Art Graphics, Regents Park Road London NW1.

Printed by Stamford Press Pte Ltd

Swan Hill Press

an imprint of Quiller Publishing Ltd

Wykey House, Wykey, Shrewsbury, SY4 1JA, England
Tel: 01939 261616 Fax: 01939 261606
E-mail: info@quillerbooks.com
Website: www.swanhillbooks.com

Acknowlegements

———◆———

My unbounded thanks to *The Shooting Gazette*, and to its sainted Editor-in-Chief Mike Barnes in particular, for having published the following articles (or even parts of them) over the past years. I am eternally grateful for his kindness, faith and generosity, and for allowing me such unique opportunities and privileges.

In order to ensure that neither he, nor *The Shooting Gazette* magazine, suffer any repercussions, outraged correspondence or ugly comebacks as a result of this publication of which they have so generously approved, I would like to make it perfectly clear that all opinions, sentiments, viewpoints or presumptions, as well as all factual errors and any generally nonsensical twaddle, are *not* the responsibility of, nor indeed remotely mirror any of the opinions and principles held by, the magazine or its editors, but are mine alone.

I am very grateful to General Isles for allowing his letter to be reprinted.

My greatest affection and gratitude go to Donald Stewart – my very dear friend and my companion, hero, guru and mentor – for so many years of laughter, shared drams, daft moments, zany incidents and an indescribable amount of sheer fun, some of which is re-lived in these pages. I must also thank my long-suffering and darling daughter, and the many friends like George Bruce, Malcolm Innes and others who, wittingly or not, have also provided me with stories or material of one sort or another.

There is no adequate way of thanking Tim Jaques for his drawings and designs, his humour and patience and his unfailing enthusiasm. To work with a friend is one thing; to have remained friends, in *spite* of working together for so long, is quite another. He is a total star.

To Mara
with all my love

Contents

———◆———

Instructions Attached

I don't know about you, but whenever I open a box with a new toy inside (I use the word 'toy' very loosely, you understand; it doesn't mean I'm actually still into Lego or Barbie dolls; it does mean something of a generally gadgetty nature, and includes everything from an emporium-sized fridge, or an underwater camera with submarine attached, to a new drill-bit, or one of those must-have little gizmos that add something even more magical to your glamorous lifestyle), I always find that it comes with a whole lot of instructions attached.

These instructions may come in sheaves or even book form ('The Manual') or they may be written out on a whole series of separate little fly-leaves that you try to clamp together like a badly-held bridge-hand and then drop, together with the other loose bits of paper like guarantee forms, disclaimer forms, consumer surveys etc. etc. and which all disappear without trace for a year or so behind the sofa, under the carpet or behind the oven.

Anywhere where you don't normally look on a daily basis anyway. And they're in every language known to man. I really like the instructions in Chinese as, if you hold them upside down, they look exactly the same as they did before. But I *especially* like the ones that have been translated into English *from* the Chinese, either by a dyslexic translator or by a baboon taking a break from banging out Hamlet on the sort of old sit-up-and-beg typewriter that you see in black and white films about Hemingway.

Like microbes, instructions are now part of daily life. Every single commercially-produced item seems to carry instructions or caveats; even books and sheet music bear copyright warnings. It's quite creepy when you start to think about it. 'Remove hanger before wearing' (drycleaners' sign); 'This packet contains nuts and may cause anaphylactic attack' (on bag of peanuts); 'Dispose of plastic packaging immediately: it can suffocate a child'; 'Now wash your hands'; 'Do not iron clothes on body' (in box containing new iron) or, in the manual with the microwave, 'Do not place live animals' (hamsters, say?) 'inside appliance'. The best one was on a Swedish chainsaw: 'Do not attempt to stop chain with hands or genitals' – now there's an idea... Being short on patience however, I usually can't be bothered to read instructions. This means that the contents of every Tetra-pack I've ever opened have invariably ended up all over the walls.

It also means that I have learned the hard way never to purchase *anything* that comes flat-packed 'for easy home assembly'. I once tried a set of shelves. They took hours to cobble together but miraculously they stayed up; so I tidied the mess, closed the door quietly behind me and began congratulating myself on having won that particular *mano a mano*, at which point they promptly and very noisily laughed and fell off the wall. I think it must be something to do with female genes: my mother didn't understand the meaning of D.I.Y. (she always thought it implied something rather seedy, probably involving self-abuse); and my daughter, having (once) tried to fit a push-chair together, obeying every single instruction to the letter, discovered that she still had two wheels and a wing spare at the end. In general, women aren't overly instruction-literate; we like to plug-and-go.

It's quite interesting, if you've got nothing better on, to try and think of anything that doesn't have instructions, warnings or conditions attached. Not counting dogs, lovers or babies – all of which ought to have manuals stapled to them – it's not a long list: jewellery; antiques; bespoke clothing; market produce; hand-made shoes; stamps; livestock; pianos, and horse-shit. And that's about it, I reckon.

Oh, and shotguns. Imagine it:-

'Open box/case. Remove stock, barrels, and fore-end, separately packed as (1), (2) & (3) [see diagram]. Discard all grease-proof paper. Take stock, no, take 'the stock' (1) & clamp widest end between R. elbow and hip. Grip trigger-guard [see (1)(c) on diagram] with R. hand. Push opening lever on top *[(1)(d) ditto]* to R. with R. thumb. *Don't let go.* Take 'barrels' (2) in L. hand, with biggest holes facing you, ensuring long thin flat bit *[aka. 'rib' – [see (1)(d)]* between barrels is uppermost [see 'This Way Up' diagram]. Carefully place chunky metal 'teeth' of (2) above square metal apertures of (1). Moving R. hip forward as guide, engage (l) and (2) together. Carefully release 1(d) and any surplus fingers and (1) and (2) should now be in line. *(If not, why not?)* Now take 'the fore-end' (3) (it's the wedge-shaped thing, dumbo) and, holding rounded top side in R., correction, L. hand, introduce bottom flanges gingerly onto (2)(z) [cf. diagram again]. Press (3) to (2) until 'clunk/click' is heard. *(If it isn't, recommence from 'Take (3)' above; please concentrate.)* WARNING: In the event of pieces of metal, spiders or detritus falling out of packaging or (1), (2), or (3), THESE MUST NOT BE SWALLOWED or your statutory rights, amongst various other things, will be affected.

NB. The Gunmakers accept no responsibility whatsoever for any personal physical or psychiatric damage or subsequent counselling incurred by you as a result of following these instructions.'

No. Mercifully, a shotgun doesn't come with instructions attached. And as far as I'm concerned, that's absolutely brilliant. I don't need to know that there are three zillion tiny buggery little twiddly bits inside – I'll be fully occupied just trying to shoot straight with the thing – but if ever I do hear the sound of knives and forks coming from within, then I'll simply send the whole caboodle back to the maker. And shotguns are just about the only things that you do (and should) regularly send back to the makers – something which doesn't apply to babies, stamps, or horse-shit. Now that *is* magic.

New Year's Diary

———————————◆———————————

January 2nd

Haven't kept up diary for yonks – too busy concentrating on really vital things like ignoring Time's Winged Chariot and worrying about Doing Something With One's Life, blah de blah de blah. ie: Muddling Through. Why does year go by so fast once you're over ten? Why am I now doing spring cleaning in autumn? What is it about trying to be domestic goddess that makes one feel weak? Have decided however that today is perfect for resolving seriously momentous matters like whether can finally write Great Booker-winning Novel (no way), whether to tackle waste-land and other people's dog messes outside back door (leave for someone else to do. Or enter for Turner prize) and most importantly whether or not to go for for Botox. On reflection, and knowing I have pain threshold of a midge, probably not. Good: that's this year sorted.

Curate's egg of a year, this last twelvemonth. Highs and lows? Lows many and various, not important in Grand Scheme but irritating: smashing face in, while trying to burgle way into own window and falling 5ft. off sill onto concrete, followed by months of heavy theatrical make-up to disguise gothic bruising which resulted in strangers at supermarket-checkout glancing quickly away and silently mouthing 'BATTERED WIFE????' to each other in queues. Usual humiliations on corporate clays. None of diets worked. And miracle creams aren't. Hey ho. Highs? Lots really, including first proper fishing lesson. (Actually, why need fishing lessons for God's sake? Or soufflé-classes? Or books on motherhood? Or videos of *Sex in the City*? How come genetic memory not enough?? NB. shooting is different.) And, thanks to said lesson, first fish – very chuffing esp. when you feel you've 'earned' it, rather like first really 'good' stag. (Or is this being a tad Presbyterian? So who cares anyway?) Oh, and found yet another great new shooting school for lessons with star guy David who told me to close one eye when they came straight over. Wow! Don't know what Sir R. F.-P.-Gallwey Bart. or other Old Masters would have said, thought you weren't allowed to. But D. says that's bollocks and whatever works for you is ok... Wish all men were so understanding. ('How was it for you darling?' 'Great so long as I kept one eye closed'. Can just see that going down a treat.)

Tried out one-eyed bit at first shoot of season. Have to admit, not exactly a *succès fou* to start with: if you shut one eye too early you lose all sense of balance and fall over. This looks pretty damned stupid if (a) you're on perfectly flat ground (b) you do it twice (c) you're in a line of over-60s as they all think you've had a seizure. Nice neighbouring guns rushed to help which entailed babbling apologies from supine position and quick thinking ('must have just twisted my ankle, NO harm done, SO sorry, SILLY me') and merry laughter all round. After a bit, got the closure-timing better and it worked... O Frabjous Day. Only problem was remembering to continue hobbling on mythical twist afterwards, to add verisimilitude to an otherwise bald and unconvincing tale.

New Year's resolution: Get Timing Right. Feel this will also be of enormous help in many other different areas of Life – most other areas in fact.

What else... In July won a day's fishing in competition draw. Amazing. Have never ever won anything in ANY sort of draw (except for small bottle of medicated shampoo, once) so great excitement. Took three chums down to frightfully up-market private bit of chalk-stream, with food, lots of booze plus books, papers etc. in case anyone got bored. Thoughtful or what? Very

pretty river, scenery, house, fishing hut, birds flitting about etc. etc., and fish galumphing all over the place. Owner away on hols but someone apparently around – burglar with smart car perhaps? – though invisible. Chums caught two fish. Day then ruined by appearance of four maniac resident Scotties who attacked mild-mannered fishing party like a pack of bloody wild-cats and savaged everyone from knees down (ok, can understand Doberman guard-dogs frothing at mouth, but SCOTTIES? Gimme a break...) Total nightmare; they actually succeeded in drawing blood from one friend who ironically had just given some the day before.

Packed up cars and left in hurry to get stitches and transfusion at local hospital. Shades of Hancock in *The Blood Donor*. And my No.1 moleskins looked like they'd been done over by rotivator. Wrote very curt letter to owner after. If we'd been rapacious foreigners he'd have been sued. Memo: take out comprehensive full-party insurance and wear thigh-boots whenever fishing ANY-WHERE in future. Come to think of it, thigh-boots quite sexy anyway, so could be in permanent demand? Hmmm. And cave all bloody little yappy things at all times, only wish I'd managed to kick one in goolies and / or river.

Best bits from past year:-

Best diet: Cut out breakfast. Cut out lunch. Cut out dinner.

Best e-mail: Radio transmission, released by US navy. Navy opens with:
A) Please divert your course 15 degrees north to avoid collision.
B) Recommend YOU divert your course 14 degrees south to avoid collision.
A) This is the captain of a US Navy vessel. I say again: divert your course.
B) Negative. I say again, divert YOUR course.
A) THIS IS THE AIRCRAFT CARRIER ENTERPRISE. WE ARE A LARGE WARSHIP OF THE US NAVY. DIVERT YOUR COURSE IMMEDIATELY.
B) This is a lighthouse. Your call.

Best travel info: In the states of Georgia, Alabama and Texas, it is legal to own a gun but not a vibrator.

In The Best Company

My first introduction to shooting with a shotgun was when I was six. We lived in Ireland, both parents shot a fair amount and I was allowed to join the party one day when they went on a foray with some friends over the snipe bogs. The Siamese cat – who always came out on these expeditions as it liked picking up – and I were tethered to each other, and there were strict instructions about keeping up, staying in line etc. The cat got something in its paw, I came to a stop, he yowled and someone whipped round accidentally letting off their gun, apparently missing me by inches. With that blind and illogical fury peculiar to maternal terror my mother let forth a torrent of abuse, directed entirely at me: it was all my fault, I might have been killed, what ever did I think I was playing at and so on, all of which seemed to be totally unfair. The upshot was that I was then forbidden to go out with the guns for, I remember, a whole year. This also seemed wholly unjust, but was a healthy preparation for later life when, as a woman in the shooting field, you are invariably blamed for everything – being in the wrong place, doing the wrong thing, or just for being a woman anyway.

Home life and its somewhat eccentric learning curves then came second to the inevitable, seemingly interminable, years of formal education. Ireland gave way to my father's postings abroad; schools in France or Cairo and convents back in England didn't encourage their gels to tote firearms. I spent a year at the Lycée in Kensington, where all the boys had knives, but it wasn't the same thing. So it wasn't until I'd come down from university and was working in London that I had my first glimpse of this exotic world, in the shape of a boyfriend whose sole passion was shooting. The first time I met him at a dinner party, he turned to me at the end and said cheerfully: 'How's about a drink at my place then? I'll show you my hammer gun.' It was, I felt, a rather novel approach.

As far as intellectual pursuits were concerned he evinced all the capabilities of a protopod, but guns, rifles, feet per second, Hawker and Ross, loads and trajectories, black powder and Manton actions – that was different. I was smitten. I rigged myself out in all the correct gear so I wouldn't disgrace him on shooting parties; studiously attended sales of arms; made all the right noises when he returned having shot 120 duck before breakfast; never complained even when rendered senseless by the cold... Then one day I announced I'd signed up for shooting lessons. BEEG mistake. All hell broke loose; there was such an outrage you'd think I'd abseiled naked into the *Curia* for God's sake. I suppose it was really dim of me but until that moment I'd never realised that shooting was apparently a Men Only sport. As any fule kno.

Now I know that men are biologically different from women in that they possess the special Y-chromosome. This is what gives them their uniquely manly attributes like great physical strength and the inability to fold a bath-towel. Shooting however is not, or should not be, a sexist issue. In general, men are taught to shoot a shotgun at an earlier age than girls, and consequently girls have to work harder than men to be accepted in the shooting field. But any girl can learn how to shoot, just as she can learn aerial combat, discounted cash flow, spot-welding – you name it. It's perfectly simple: there are only two things in life that men can do and women can't, and this isn't the time or the place to go into either of them.

Men have always hunted in

packs; it was a case of necessity. Likewise for centuries men have enjoyed the company of other men, be it in the masonry of clubs, or of coffee-houses, or the church. (The C. of E., my father always maintained, was the microcosm of English society – run by gentlemen for gentlemen.) Or indeed the shooting field. Guns were men's business which, in the early days of firearms, was fair enough. But times change and traditions too. The erstwhile Earl of Warwick was famously reputed to have complained about the advent of the lady in the shooting field, saying that he had 'met ladies who shoot, and have come to the conclusion – being no longer young and a staunch Conservative – that I would prefer them not to.'

What is most remarkable about the last few decades is that, without recourse to chaining themselves to the gun-cabinets, women have been – happily and willingly it would seem – welcomed into the field. This of course speaks volumes for the true nobility and generosity of spirit evinced by modern gentlemen of the shooting fraternity, who in earlier generations would have been aghast at the very idea. In those dark days of yore, females were undoubtedly felt to be a threat to the general machismo of the event, probably wearing little badges saying 'Sex Appeal Please Give Generously' pinned to their bosoms and frightening the birds.

Nowadays a lady gun is no longer a contradiction in terms. Although she must never of course forget her place (she should try and shoot as well as, but never on any account better than, the gentlemen *for* whom after all, and by whom, the sport was conceived); and if she can, safely and cleanly, pull down the high birds with the best of them, her male companions will be the first to purr and congratulate her, the ultimate accolade.

After all, it's a matter of companionship and of participation, not of gender. Although how the Earl of Warwick would have greeted the intelligence that ladies have now been admitted to The Worshipful Company of Gunmakers, I dread to imagine.

Worried Silly

———◆———

I suppose it's simply another irritating female trait, but I know that I do worry excessively. I put it down entirely to genes however: my mother worried about everything and anything, all the time – it was almost a professional hobby and she went at it like a terrier with a bone: the political situation, the lack of soft loo paper in museums, the price of postage-stamps, global warming, broken glass in the rubbish, the demise of proper enunciation in the BBC, refugees, everything was grist to the mill. When nothing else sprang to mind she'd revert to her favourite chestnut, the parlous state of her only child's immortal soul; at which point my father and I would turn on her. 'Come on darling, you're getting idle – there must be something more challenging – what about abortion? or the FTSE? or bush fires, or the American elections? What about the Latin Mass or the life span of lightbulbs for heaven's sake?' She'd giggle and sigh thankfully. 'You know, you're quite right' she'd say, and off she'd go again onto something else. A real goer, my mother.

I'm not so globally philanthropic with my anxieties. I'm more your self-centered, pathologically introverted worrier, only concerned with things that affect me personally. Why does a 2lb box of chocolates make me gain 5lb? My daughter's at least seven minutes late – what if she's had an accident?... When I'm a grandmother will I be any good? Now that I've sat on the grass, will I have stains on my bum or get piles? Or both? I wonder if I've sorted out all the things I'm going to need for going away next week/month/year, plus all the other stuff that I don't yet know I'll need, but will undoubtedly need at some point... How come all my clothes shrink a size when I put them away? Did I remember to close the windows in the house before I drove off, so the squirrels can't get in and squitter on the sofas? What happens if the car catches fire on the motorway? Come to think of it, where did I park the thing anyway? A stranger at the door, must be a rapist...Maybe I'm getting dementia...does somebody tell you? And now I've forgotten where I put the list of

things I've got to remember to do, and that's seriously worrying.

There's always something to worry about. Even the most innocuous things can be fraught with worry. For instance, people are kind and sweet and generous, and they ask you to come and stay, and that's wonderful. Sometimes, it's a shooting invitation too, and they'll tell you where it'll be etc. so you know the form. That's lovely. Sometimes, although it's not a shooting invitation as such, they're just asking you to stay the weekend which will be delicious anyway; but also, just possibly, there might be the odd chance of a shot at something... So right at the very end of the conversation, they add: 'Oh and by the way, just in case we decide to go pottering out for the odd pigeon or something in the evening, don't bother about squibs or anything, just fling in a gun...'

JUST FLING IN A GUN? Whaddyamean, *just fling* in a gun? What they don't realize of course is that it takes me a good five days of apprehension, agony and anxiety for any invitation that involves shooting. As it is, merely an invitation to 'come and spend the weekend', and I begin packing three days before. A weekend *shooting* invitation, and I'm worried silly there laying things out come Monday night...

And, for the really committed worrier such as myself, shooting is the most wonderfully rich vein to tap. The list of things to fret over is almost endless: whether I'm going to get to the appointed place; where's the map – did I remember to fill the car with petrol yesterday? And, if by some miracle I manage to do so, and on time, will there be plenty of time to spare and a loo? What will I find I've left behind? Can I remember the mnemonic I worked out for the Really Vital Seven Items ? Ah yes: '*Gorgeous Girls Can Easily Be Hot Shots*' (for 'Gun, Gloves, Cartridges, Ear-defenders, Boots, Hat, Stick' of course – good, that; rather like Moh's Measurement of Harness scale for minerals, going from talc up to diamond: *Tall Girls Can F*** And Other Queer Things Can Do,* ha ha, where was I...) What about all the other stuff , like gunslip / cartridge-bag / contact lenses / shotgun certificate / game licence / extra lenses / spare batteries for ear-defenders / tip-money etc. etc. etc.? If the sun's out and low in the eyes, sunglasses? If it rains, have I got waterproof everything including mascara? If it snows will nose and cheeks go usual luminous red, making one look like Russian doll between drives? Are hair brush, shoes for lunch and spare make-up all in magic truffle-hunter's handbag? And insurance papers?

Will I, God forbid, let off what might even be vaguely construed as a greedy shot at someone else's bird? And – marginally worse – if it's one of those dreaded Cocks Only day, *will I be able to tell* (and if not, how the hell do you explain bringing down something else – a small hang-glider or a pterodactyl for instance – by mistake? Light laugh? I think not...hara-kiri more likely.) And – the most agonising of all anxieties – will I manage to hit anything all, or will the cartridge-to-bird ratio yet again resemble an Australian cricket score (like, say, 198 for 2) and if it is, will they ever ask me back?

All the stuff is piled up in mountain-ranges by the front door. Which reminds me – spade for snowdrifts. In case. Horrendous amount: more gear, kit and clobber, bags and baggage... even the *Roi Soleil, chaise percée* and all, got by with less. And I bet I've still forgotten something... And this is just for what is supposed to be nothing more complicated than a jolly day out shooting with friends. Stupid? Not me, sweet pea. I believe that worrying about things constructively and *thoughtfully*, as I obviously do, actually helps you – either by preparing you for the worst, or by reminding you to try and ensure it doesn't happen. Anyway it's a very good theory and for the sake of general world peace I'm sticking to it. It does however make one impatient with other people who worry just for the sake of it, like my mother did, and who are obviously bored out of their skulls and have nothing else to do with their time and who would be far better off getting to grips with something *really* useful like completing the daily crossword or working out the periodic table of elements in order of atomic numbers or proof-reading those mad English versions of foreign menus...

It takes one to know one of course. Driving along a nice country road in Scotland some months ago, the mind in neutral and all well with the world, I saw a sign on the gate of a field which read NO WORRYING SHEEP. Well, I caught myself thinking, that's great and thank heavens; but what on earth would they be worried about anyway?

After a Fashion

———◆———

It had been a wonderful day at the grouse: weather gorgeous, wind just right and birds in their hundreds. Very hard work, but hugely satisfying. At the end of the final drive, he turns to his new young wife (they're actually – such is the harmony between them – on their honeymoon at this point): 'You know, old thing' he says happily, 'I've just twigged – who needs women when you've got all this?'

Given the fact that she is vivacious, stunning and South American, I couldn't understand why she hadn't disembowelled him on the spot or, indeed, how she was still with him twenty-two years later. 'Although I'd been educated over here' she explained, 'it's very hard marrying an Englishman who shoots. I didn't know anything about shooting – they didn't teach us that at Winkfield. But you learn, of course. These days I don't worry so much about what to wear, and now I've got a dog he's perfectly happy for me to come along.'

I just don't understand it. Unlike the continentals, English shooting men are deeply and inherently misogynistic; they basically just don't *like* women around when they're in the field – in any capacity. A Frenchman, say, is never happier than when surrounded by women – the more the merrier – and will chunner away blithely to them before, during and after every drive and even probably find a reason to stop for a little dalliance between coverts. Englishmen speak, in monosyllables, only to each other or to their dogs. If there must be a female around she should be silent, biddable and preferably labrador (so if he barks 'Lie DOWN dammit', ON NO ACCOUNT should you do so – *he won't be talking to you*.) A woman is there for utility not adornment, and definitely not as a sex object. Hence she should never, of course, look glamorous – it only distracts everybody. 'Glamour' is not a word heard in the shooting field in this country.

So, none of the 'Ah Fifi, my leedle passion-flower, ow abert we luk at the *agenda de chasse* for dis yar? An pairaps zen a veezeet to Hermes or Purrday, for some *chic* closes for yu for ze seezon, *non?'* An Englishman, balefully suffering the wife's perennial cry of despair ('But I haven't a THING to wear') regards any expenditure on shooting clothes (especially hers) as total lunacy. He's inherited all his grandfather's kit, why does she need anything new? 'What?... o I dunno... erm... for heaven's sake woman, you've got those old cords you do the hens in haven't you? Whadyamean you burned 'em? Seemed perfectly fine to me – dammit it's a shoot you're going on, not a catwalk.'

Mind you it's jolly hard to look chic as a woman out shooting in this country. You can't wear lovely long leather skirts and full-length fox coats as you can in Belgium, as the dogs get over-excited and you'll get shot the minute you go behind a bush. You can't wear *un petit tweed anglais* and proper leather walking shoes with little tassels in front as they do in France as you'll get sodden and disappear without trace in a ditch. In Spain the girls all dress in marvellous frilly-fronted bull-fighters' shirts and huge hats and fringed-riding chaps. Don't even *think* of crossing a barbed wire

fence in England in fringes and no crotch – it really can make the eyes water.

It was all very well in Edwardian days when, as a spectator, a lady had to do no more than sit quietly, sport a fetching rig and be decorative. Now, life's a bit different. 'Pay attENtion will you – and take those silly things off you can't possibly load properly wearing gloves... Ahh – here we go – MARK IT... hell... no just LEAVE... Oh for Pete's sake there's no time to sit down now...' No time either to admire the scenery or flirt with the other players, even when the drive's over. 'It came down over THERE... well, go ON then, I've got more than enough to pick up here... what? I KNOW it's over the river... well you should have just worn them should-n't you, HURRY UP we haven't got all day...' So, whether as a spec-tator or a shot, you have to be Properly Turned Out (the essence of good dressing after all); and if that means wearing rubber boots and the sort of hat that makes you look like a drowned moose and the waterproof jacket and the tweeds that can be cobbled togeth-er and won't show the blood after you have been ripped to shreds catching one of his sodding runners in the holly hedge, so be it. It's a uniform after all and, whether you're shooting or not, it makes you look professional and as if you know what you're doing and it looks 'correct'. It won't help you pull, but you can live with that, for a day anyway.

Unless of course you're a really good shot, when you can be a little more adventurous. 'Ladies' Days' (the women shoot; admir-ers, but never husbands, may come and admire) are a god-send for learning how to retain every ounce of feminine chic as a lady gun. There's lots of girl-talk too – the sort men really hate – on the lines of 'gosh-that's-pretty-where-*did*-you-get-it?' and not just referring to the tanned 6ft Chippendale the hostess is wearing today as a wrap.

But you still have to dress 'appropriately' as a shot, otherwise you look ridiculous. It's all very well wearing tight suede pants and being swathed in long cashmere scarves with good earrings under large hat if you're going to sit on a leather tripod seat and spectate; it's not good for shooting in. I tried it once: scarf acts as whiplash, getting wrapped firmly round barrels and boots; hat takes off removing ear-defenders with it; earring gets stuck in extractor; then tripod, which you'd think was minding its own business quietly on the side, goes for soft underbelly in sneaky low-level attack and you're felled in thick plough. Suede pants a write-off.

I did once see a girl shooting on the west coast of Scotland, wearing a long tweed skirt and pretty little leather buttoned boots, like Victorian skating boots really – adorable. As outside gun on the last drive (the sea-drive it was called: the birds were pushed off some crops some 300 yards above the shore, and flew out like starlings before climbing and turning back home) she was despatched to the end of the line, which meant navigating across the rocks and pools and making for a small sandy spur jutting out into the sea. Halfway through the drive, the tide began to come in behind her. And you really *cannot* shoot properly standing full fathoms five in pretty little leather buttoned boots, clutching the hem of your skirt firmly between your teeth. It just *doesn't* look professional somehow.

Hit and Miss

———◆———

I'd give anything not to have pre-shoot nerves. I spend the entire night before a shoot waking at hourly intervals, panicking that the alarm has gone off and I've missed it; arrive at breakfast with bags the size of portmanteaux under the eyes and so have to wear shades over the bacon and eggs (which does look pretty stupid), and then have to hyperventilate into a paper bag before the first drive. It's hell. And the first drive is hell too as the first bird invariably comes slap over you – it always happens, doesn't it – and you have to make your mind up in that split second of decision-time (1) whether it's the right species for the day; (2) whether (if it's a Cocks Only day) it is a cock and (3) whether it's going to be worse to miss it, which you know you're bound to, or to throw up publicly, or just do the one followed by the other. I'm a great guest to have at a shoot, I can tell you. Pathetic really. It's only when you confess to it later on that you realise that a lot of people go through the same terrors, (although rarely to the same debilitating degree) and are just thanking their lucky stars it's not their turn to suffer that particular public humiliation.

There are also the other sort of public humiliations, the ones that everyone else finds hilarious. Like some joker has substituted one of the cartridges in your belt or pocket for another which has had all the shot taken out of it and replaced with flour. And in the heat of a mind-blowing drive you take a thoughtful, really concentrated shot at some old cock bird screaming off a 300-foot bank and there's a click, and nothing happens. Funny, that – must be a misfire; and suddenly you're being smothered in this huge cloud of white stuff and choking to *death* for God's sake and the whole line, who've been wait-

ing for it to happen, are having hysterics.

Sometimes, though, missing is not all that funny. Especially when it's with a rifle. Every shot you've ever missed with a rifle (probably because you're very likely to only have one single chance, and then you're sent home in disgrace) you remember for ever.

I'd been asked to stalk chamois in Austria. I'd arrived late in the evening – too late to go and try out the rifle I was going to be lent for the next day's dawn sortie. It's always a mistake not to be able to zero a rifle yourself: you need to get the feel of it, what the trigger-pull is like (although you can do that bit 'dry'), where it shoots, whether the sights need altering a bit to suit you and so forth, before you use the thing in earnest. However my host, a stern man in the Prussian mode, would have none of it. No, I couldn't sight it first thing in the morning either; it was *his* rifle, he'd never missed a beast with it, he sincerely hoped I was able to shoot properly as he would be taking me out himself, end of discussion and goodnight.

Talk about pre-shoot nerves. All night long the enormous

porcelain stove in the corner of my tiny freezing room groaned and belched, and I know I only had twenty minutes' sleep all told. Dawn broke to find us climbing Everest. (OK, but when you've had a night like that, almost anything feels like Everest.) We climbed for over three hours in unbroken silence, and I was already regretting what was clearly going to be a tricky exercise. Finally, we came to a halt. A speck in the distance, and there was a chamois dancing on the top of a rock about a mile away, which is what chamois do. We took another two hours climbing, navigating across rockfaces and climbing yet again to get within range, then my host turned and handed me the rifle. ('Off kors, yoo shood be carrying ziz yoorself. Tooday, I vill carry for yoo as yoo are a vumman' he'd spat out as we'd set off.) I peered through the telescope and nudged the safety-catch off. 'Will I aim up a bit?' I whispered. (Always better to ask, if you're not 100% certain of the distance, and this was unfamiliar and deceptive terrain.)

'Zertainly nott' was the curt response. 'Zis rifle shoods purfectly flet for sreehunredfiftee meters. Aim for ze hart.' I aimed for the heart.

The shot cracked out, the mountains echoed, and the chamois looked round curiously. I had re-loaded immediately. 'HAH, yoo MIZT' hissed my host furiously and, I thought, a trifle unneccessarily. 'Yoo flinched. Shood again.' Carefully, I shot again. Zippo. 'AHA, *ja*, yoo FLINCHED.' 'I'm sorry' I said, meaning it; 'but I did *not* flinch; I know perfectly well when I flinch, and I didn't flinch.' '*Ja ja*, yoo flinched. I haff ZEEN yoo flinch. Give me ze rifle, I vill shood ze beezt.' He snatched the rifle from me, slammed at the safety-catch, aimed and squeezed the trigger. The echo was deafening. I thought of England and wanted to die of shame.

In spite of all this noise the chamois seemed totally unperturbed. (Perhaps it thought it was a mountain storm. Perhaps it just wasn't very bright. At any rate, there was no reaction.) Unlike the firer who swore impressively, and fired yet again. Same result. I started to feel much better. The chamois finally woke up, looked across at us and, suddenly alert, turned and flounced off across the peaks. Neither of us said a word.

We returned down to the lodge, a three-hour walk, still in total silence. Immediately upon arrival, my host produced a large piece of white paper, made an aiming mark in the middle with a bit of dirt and pinned it up on a target about a hundred meters away. Having still not been spoken to, I stood and watched. He lay down, loaded the rifle again and fired at the paper. The hole was about a foot high from the aiming mark and eight inches left. He turned to me, scarlet in the face. 'Yoo ZEE' he yelled murderously, 'YOO ZEE ZAT, yoo haff knocked ze sights YOO SCHTOOPID VUMMAN, yoo haff knocked ze SIGHTS.' I thought about this for a moment. 'Well' I replied (cautiously – you can never tell with people who suffer from high blood-pressure – but I was damned if I was going to be accused and then not allowed to speak): 'I don't *think* I could have done that; you see, you very kindly carried the rifle the whole way for me, if you remember...'

That afternoon, I was allowed to zero the rifle under the stern eye of a keeper, with whom I went out the next morning. We had a very nice stalk and returned with a chamois in the rucksack. The incident was never referred to again.

Sporting Adornments

———◆———

Jewellery is one thing a woman can wear at all times; most women have a 'Presents for any occasion' list which just consists of the words 'rocks and La Perla, please'. Even out shooting, it is not considered bad form for a girl to sport a ring or two so long as they don't interfere with the triggers, although earrings are usually not recommended as they get caught up in the ear-defenders. But latterly, it has to be said, I was beginning to feel rather *passée* in the adornment stakes. Not quite up to snuff, a little *demodée* even. The reason for this was simple: I was not socially studded – that facial or body-accessory sported not only by the denizens of the Bikes R Us brigade and the *boulevardiers* of Essex and what is termed 'sarf of ve river', but also greatly in evidence now amongst some of the younger *Hello* or Badminton set. Neither did I boast what is now considered *de rigueur* in the smarter social magazines and designer chic – a tattoo. This grave fashion omission would obviously have to be rectified.

Not, I hasten to add, that I was proposing to have a stud inserted *anywhere* at all on my person, thank you very much. But a tattoo, now that might just be the job, and confirm my standing, finally, as one of the Beautiful People... After all, come to think of it, it was discovered, immediately after the battle of Hastings, that King Harold was amongst the fore-runners of fashion, having had the name 'Edith' engraved onto his arm; frankly therefore, what was good enough for the king, then, should be good enough for me, now.

The design of the prospective tattoo was naturally going to be of paramount importance. Nothing like 'muvver' or 'coobritannia' or a heart and anchor – nothing coarse or remotely reminiscent of the building site. Something fine and discreet – a very small mouse somewhere, or a butterfly down the *décolletage* perhaps...? No – on second thoughts, neither of these were really 'me' – the obvious point of the thing being that you really have to choose a design which reflects your own personal taste and interests, and also suits your personality and, quite importantly, your body if you are going to have the whole works.

Now although no-one in their right mind could ever describe me as 'petite', a Full Corporate Image of my personal interests (a depiction of a rolling wooded landscape would be nice, with a couple of flat-coats and a spaniel in the foreground sitting patiently by their gun, and pheasants high in the sky and partridges appearing over a bush – no, a hedgerow – out of a low winter sun, together with a river and a hill with some deer in the background), although only marginally OTT, would surely be considered a full body job. This was probably veering towards overkill however, and also might well cause some raised eyebrows at the next black tie do – the Gunmakers Livery dinner perhaps? Although they do specify that 'Decorations will be worn'... And moreover, would I then have any private areas whatsoever left *intacta* after such a full-scale *oéuvre*? Added to which, the cost would be prohibitive. In that case however, perhaps I could try and get sponsorship by an interested countryside/sporting body; but would they then demand – and they would be perfectly within their rights to do so as part of their advertising strategy, those publicity boys are ruthless – that, say, I go and stand naked on a plinth at the next Game Fair, or in the Tate Modern or the Summer Exhibition? Added to these disturbing possibilities was the thought that such a momentous work of art would require weeks of hospitalisation to undertake, and would probably ruin not only my bank balance but also any of my last remaining chances.

A taxing problem, which contrived both to exercise and to amuse for, I confess, some considerable time. However the final solution to what had been, at the start, a simple and undoubtedly brilliant idea, was swiftly reached after I emerged from daydream mode and realised one very simple fact: I actually hate tattoos, and would undoubtedly loathe mine within about two seconds of its completion. Better, surely, far simpler in the end, painless and costing less than a second-class stamp, to settle for one of those easy, peel-off, water-resistant numbers, rather like a small piece of Sellotape, from a party-shop. Good thinking. But as to the design, that now became more difficult to decide on, as none of the commercially-available ones fitted my particular, albeit rather idiosyncratic, bill. I didn't want dragons or flowers or

sports-cars, or devils or dolphins, or banners announcing Love Is
Free or balloons or Snoopy – what I *really* wanted was something
like a very small version of the Game Conservancy logo which
would have been just the ticket, but they hadn't got one in their
catalogue. So I searched around for several weeks and finally
found, and bought, a tiny and rather charming fake, stick-on tattoo, about half an inch long, depicting a feather.

My new acquisition is a triumph and I am extremely pleased
with it. I can bathe in it, party in it, shoot in it and, best of all,
remove it instantly – painlessly and with no after-effects – whenever I want. It looks very pretty and is, furthermore, invisible to
the world at large. And I'm certainly not telling anyone where it
is.

Trials and Tribulations

———————◆———————

There are certain dates in the year that you really look forward to. When you're five, it's Christmas; when you're nine, it's being ten; when you're older, it's the last day of school, ever, and after that it depends on what your interests are, the things that are really important... the first race-meeting of the year, the Summer Exhibition preview at the R.A, the first run down in fresh snow, the opening day on the river, the Twelfth... Me, I look forward to February 2nd.

No, it's not my birthday or a saint's day or, *strictly* speaking, a day of any significance in anyone's calender but my own. And I look forward to it passionately because it will be the first day for six and a half months that I shall be able to wake up, perfectly rested from a deep and untroubled sleep, since August the previous year.

It's this recurring nightmare I keep having, doctor – from the moment the shooting season begins. Same each time: I've just driven somewhere for a day's shooting, arrived at the meeting-place, friends milling around and I'm unpacking the car boot. Yes, remembered the mantra, everything's there – jackets, boots, socks; shooting gloves; ear-defenders, batteries. Spare batteries. Scarf, hat, small bits of plaster for when I close my trigger-finger in the breech. Tip for head-keeper, credit card for petrol. Full cartridge bag, gunslip, spare cartridges. Guncase. Whew. Unstrap gun-case and open up. *Empty*. Bang goes yet another night's sleep.

The best-laid plans do get screwed up occasionally, though it's marginally worse when it happens during normal waking hours. We were up at home in Scotland, it was February 15th, the last day of the hind season. Only seven more to get to complete the cull quota, three stalking parties would go out, keeping in touch by radio so everyone would know what everyone else was doing, as hinds very thin on the ground by then. Good, efficient planning. (Better by far to have got them all by Christmas of course, which is what most intelligent lairds do, but there you are, can't have everything all the time.) The other two parties had drawn a total

blank all day so had joined up with Donald and me, who'd got four. Suddenly, we almost walked into what must have been the last bunch of hinds on the hill, tucked down in a hollow.

We all lay spying for ages, trying to decide which ones to take and who would take them. 'Tell you what' whispered Donald, 'take one each, and yous all three fire together, right? Get out the rifles. Now: you sir, you take that beast there just showing beyond yon wee lump; and Mr David'll take the one next to her and you mum, you'll take that old pale bitch in the lee just below them, that way ah can keep an eye on all three... get ready – hell they must've seen us, they're startin' to shift...best hurry...on the word 'three' then: one, two, THREE' and the three shots rang out as one. Each of us looked up and smiled at the others. 'Got yours?' 'Yep – you?' 'So did I.' 'Me too – great. Hey, what's the matter with Donald?'

Donald, who'd been lying between us all with his binoculars trained on the beasts as we'd fired, was now flat on his back, a red spotted handkerchief stuffed into his mouth, making throttled noises. 'Christ, Donald, you ok?' He sat up, removed the handkerchief and wiped his eyes with it. 'By jinxs yuz can all shoot straight, I'll give ye that' he gurgled. 'Tell you what, collect up the gear an' come over while I do the gralloching – yuz can all talk me through it.' We retrieved sticks, rifle slips and other paraphernalia and, rifles slung over shoulders, strode off after him, chatting nineteen to the dozen – an efficient, happy team. There under the hill lay a single hind, with three perfectly-placed shots in her, pole-axed.

Mind you it's a serious sport, shooting, and you shouldn't laugh about it. Imagine then (before we're done) a worst-case scenario. You've been invited to go big-game hunting. You have spent months preparing for this as you have been offered the amazing, rare opportunity to shoot a tiger. Finally the call comes: there's a rogue one they want culled. You fly half-way round the world, arrive and settle in camp, talk and think of nothing else for three days. The third night, you and the hunter creep out into the forest. A goat has been tied under a tree as bait. You both climb into a second tree and hide; you wait, for hours; nothing happens; the moon comes out; you wait several more hours; still nothing happens; the anticipation is almost unbearable.

Suddenly he's there – a shadow out of nowhere – silent, slinking towards the bait… he's on it now… the tension, the nerves, the danger – the least sound from you and that's it – your heart beating so loud surely he can hear it; wordlessly, the hunter gives you the pre-arranged 'ok' sign; here we go, safety off CAREFULLY… breathe in, breathe out then half in, now for it – and you squeeze off the shot… The world explodes, and there's the goat lying dead under the tree.

This was not a dream. I know the man who did it.

Seasonal Depression

Earlier this month, I happened to be discussing with the artist, in an uncontentious but mournful manner, the passing of time, and how I really hated February when everything just shut down: shooting things with feathers had stopped, the weather was foul, everyone got hit by S.A.D. disease, dysphoria, increased weight and low libido and it seemed like there was nothing to do except wait for life to resume some semblance of normality in May. 'Nonsense' cried the artist, never one to let a negative vibe pass by unchallenged. 'What utter rubbish. February is the month when an Englishman examines his tackle'. Eh?

I said I *thought* that that sort of thing was probably best done rather *privately* – you know, like – um – possibly in the bathroom? And anyway people I knew didn't really talk about it too much, although I had read that Syrian hamsters are sexually active only if there are a minimum of 12.5 hours of sunlight a day, which would of course cut out February... 'No no don't be idiotic – *fishing* tackle for God's sake – got a whole month to knit flies and sort out lines and all that stuff, ready for March.' Ahhh... I see... And Englishmen do that every year? A sort of male, spring-induced, kinda Ratty-on-the-riverbank thing is it? 'Oh for heaven's sake stop being obtuse – it's just something Englishmen *do* then. You women are eyeing up the Spring Collections, we're tidying out the fly boxes'. The trouble with the artist is that, as well producing canvasses, graphic designs, books and illustrations (*inter* a lot of alia), he is also a tiresomely able fisherman and shot, which means one can't argue from a position of any sort of strength. And of course only an Englishman could produce that sort of remark and make it sound as if it were Holy Writ.

What other nationalities do in February is, as *Il Duce* used to say, an Eleusinian mystery. Any French and Austrians who aren't into field sports and shooting boar are still thinking about the *pistes*, Spaniards are deep into orange crops and how the forthcoming season's *toros de lidio* are shaping up, the northerners are presumably still hibernating, the Germans are being measured up for new politicians and leather trews and heaven knows what the Italians are up to. But it is, after all, the time of year when the European sporting fraternity migrate to other continents to hunt (although in Spain, February was always, traditionally, the opening of the blackbird season). And if you're not going to Kamchatka for sheep or Cuba for snipe or Patagonia for duck or Argentina for stags, then of course there's always the spring Shooting Fair at Reno where, even though you're not actually shooting anything, you can talk endlessly about it in a testosterone-induced manner and compare trophy sizes – the sort of venue in which the statement 'mine's forty-two inches' doesn't make anyone even blink.

But for those not in travelling mode, this annual depression manifests itself in different ways. Whilst God's Chosen Few happily sort out their rod boxes, the rest of us gloomily enumerate, as in the confessional, our sins of omission and commission during the past shooting season. Forgive me Father for I have sinned: I was vain enough not to have worn enough sweaters as I felt fatter than normal and thus caught double pneumonia and therefore shot like a drain for two months ... I did not spend enough time at the shooting school, or practise my swing in the sitting room nightly. I confess also to rage, despair and a rather worrying amount of bad language in the field, not to mention the sins of pride and coveting my neighbour's shot.

A friend, whom I was boring one evening about this sort of thing, told me a sobering tale which put things instantly into perspective and proved that other people have problems far in excess of one's own petty troubles. Years ago, it was the custom in France for the President to hold an annual shoot out at Rambouillet in November, to which the most important of the country's guests and dignitaries were invited for the weekend. As with all really smart French shooting parties, the hospitality was stupendous: the castle was alive with liveried servants, the white-tie dinner was a lavish gastronomic triumph, the finest vintages flowed, the ladies were divine in all their jewels, the conversation was brilliant, the musicians played – you get the drift.

Late next morning, after a gargantuan shooting breakfast and more wine, the party sallies forth in tremendous high spirits and expectations for the first drive. Women in pretty hats and furs, laughter, scores of loaders and dogs and attendants, and the line of guns stand waiting. The park looks glorious in the pale winter sunlight. They wait.

Nothing happens. Nothing continues to happen for over half an hour. Finally the head keeper is summoned and, after a further lengthy delay, appears at last. Evidently extremely agitated, he approaches the President, bows low and is heard to whisper the immortal words: *'Desolé, Monsieur le President, mais les faisans ne sont pas encore arrivés de Paris'.*

This gave rise to the following letter in the *Shooting Gazette:*

Dear Sir,
I was somewhat amused to read Piffa Schroder's repeat of the old chestnut about the non-arrival of the birds in time for the start of the French President's grand shoot at Rambouillet.
In the early 1960s, when I was Assistant Military Attaché at our Paris Embassy the story was different but similar. It ran that HE The Ambassador was invited by General de Gaulle to the shoot at Rambouillet and, on taking the train, he observed to his astonishment the pheasants being loaded into the guard's van of his train. Both versions, I am sure, are apocryphal.

Major-General D. E. Isles CB OBE DL
Grantham, Linconshire

Deaf to all Entreaties

O ne of the things I noticed when I first went to Bisley many, many years ago, even before I'd fired my first shot with a Match Rifle, was how everyone there, whenever you spoke to them, always stood with his head facing a little away from you. This was, apparently, in no way meant to be rude – it was just 'one of those things' and merely ensured that his 'good ear' was to the fore. Which basically meant that everyone, but everyone, in camp was deaf.

So I then asked my mentor, whose knowledge and opinion on any aspect of this arcane art could be taken as dogma, why no-one seemed to wear ear-defenders for shooting Match Rifle. 'Ear-defenders?' he cried in horror. 'Good heavens no. Absolutely not. Not officers' kit at all. Match Rifle is a Gentleman's sport – not like the other disciplines, you understand; and Gentlemen don't wear ear-defenders. What Gentlemen wear is a bit of four b'two in their ears – here, look, this is how you have to do it', and that was that. I came away from my first-ever competition, lying on the firing point at 1000 yards with 70 or 80 other people blazing away, all of us with our bits of four b'two gaily fluttering in the breeze, in agony; and promptly decided that (not being a Gentleman) I was immediately going to acquire some proper, working, ear-defenders from Fulton's. Nowadays of course, thanks to health-and-safety and suchlike, everyone wears them, which only goes to show how mistaken some Gentlemen can be.

In the main, all shooting men are deaf. Especially the older ones who wouldn't ever have been caught dead in the shooting field wearing anything poncy in their ears (their grandfathers didn't after all, did they now?) and who are all now, consequently – rather like their old shooting dogs – the very devil to deal with. I know that deafness is a terrible and serious affliction, and we must all be as understanding and kind as possible, but these fellows don't help at all: they are in no sense of the word biddable, don't respond to even the most basic of hand-signals, and have certainly never learned to lip-read. And you have to keep on explaining away their 'hmm? hmm?'s too… 'SO sorry, such a bore, umm, don't I know it, but he's done an awful lot of shooting in his time, sure you understand…'; and people are very kind and everyone tries to keep their patience going and not just end up screaming 'YOU STUPID OLD FART WHY DON'T YOU GET AN EAR TRUMPET?'

There was one incident I remember with my father, who, having spent the war in the desert and thereafter, to the impotent fury of his family, resolutely and absolutely refused either to do anything about his lack of hearing, or even to contemplate trying out a hearing-aid, was as deaf as an adder. It was about six in the morning, we had just got off the night-sleeper together at

Edinburgh and, before collecting the hired car, we decided to have breakfast in the station hotel. A nice young waitress sat us down and proceeded to encourage us to order. I hadn't slept all that well on the train and mumbled something about just coffee, please, and kept my head down. She then turned to my father, who beamed.

'An' wha' about yew sur? Would yous be takin' a continen'al or a fule breakfast today?'

My father nodded enthusiastically. 'That's right' he said cheerfully; 'we've just come off the night train, hmm?'

'Em, yes sur, o' course ye have. Would yous be wantin' kippers or porridge sur?'

My father, usually a man of the utmost tolerance, affability and good humour, started to fidget uncomfortably. 'Certainly not' he replied with dignity. 'I shall pay cash.'

She gave it one more go, taking it a little slower, and with a fraction more emphasis on the important words. 'Right sur, would that be *coffee*, or *tea*, yu'd be wantin'?'

My father, now obviously feeling he was being deliberately misunderstood, lost patience. 'No, NO' he bellowed, causing a couple at the next table to jump, drop their spoons and stare round at us. 'For heaven's sake girl, we want BREAKFAST, and we'd like it NOW, right?... *If* you please...' he added, very properly. 'Funny that' he confided to me later, 'simply *wouldn't* take the order, thank heavens you sorted her out darling, otherwise we'd have been here till midday... What?... really?... oh dear...how awful...'

Shooting lunches are in a league of their own. 'I say I'm frightfully sorry,' each of your neolithic neighbours roars at you happily 'but you've got my bad side, hmmm, all right?' And you know it won't be, and you've got a good hour stuck at the cold far end of the trestle table between two dinosaurs, and it's hopeless to try shouting as they're both rumbling away to the people on their other sides while all their mildewed superannuated dogs are hogging the fire or steaming and farting under the table under everyone's feet, and it's going to be about

34

as much fun as being trapped between juggernauts in a traffic jam. Shooting dinner parties can be even worse, as they're longer, although the dogs by now have dried off and are lowering under the sideboard, and the likelihood that both your neighbours are totally stoners is marginally less (unless your hostess dislikes you and wants to make the point); so you just have to make a pact with the one who isn't, that he'll take care of you and not leave you gazing into your plate every other course. By and large, shooting men don't make very good dining companions.

Deaf dogs are interesting. They put on this I'm-sorry-but-I'm-really-extremely-busy-right-now look and totally ignore you and cover you in humiliation. But then they usually employ what is known in the trade as 'selective deafness' – rather like husbands, actually. A rabbit whisking out of the undergrowth is likely to bring this on in the first case; a perfectly innocent request for – say – a hand with the washing-up brings it on in the second. But it's funny how even the most recalcitrant of dogs can hear the crackle of a sweet-paper at half a mile; or an ancient retainer, whose lack of hearing is legendary when you're asking nicely for a drop more of that wonderful claret ('Poor old Aspic, can't hear a sausage, says it was something that happened in the Great War') is suddenly and miraculously alert and palpitating at the merest frou-frou of a folding bank-note on the other side of a closed baize door…

Men look sheepish when accused of selective deafness. Dogs too, but in their case there are known cures, although the remedies seem to vary enormously, both in efficacy and style. I once asked a Norfolk keeper how he dealt with it in his dogs.

'Arr well see' he said slowly, 'moy faaather, 'ee 'ad the roit oydeer, quoit simple reely. 'Eed joost stann there, not makin' a sownd, an' boy an' boy, the dog'ud cum back. An' moy faaather'd start torkin' to the dog, all low loike, an' sayin' things loike "*CLEverrr*" an' "*'ere then boyo*", an' 'ee'd wait until the dog'ud cum roit oop to 'im.'

'And then what did he do?'

'Arr well, then 'ee 'it 'im, dinnee? Worked every toime.'

Could work on husbands too, come to think of it.

Age of Consent

———◆———

Partridges pair off by the end of January; pheasants lay their eggs in April; red deer drop their calves, in Argyll anyway, during the third week of June and salmon spawn as you set your watch. And, handily, opening dates and the close seasons remain the same year after year. So there's a time for living and a time for dying and it's all very biblical and, in the natural world in which farmers, biologists and naturalists work, gratifyingly predictable.

However, for the average punter, there are fewer absolute laws. You get a key when you're twenty-one and a bus-pass when you're sixty and that's about it. The age of consent for all manner of things seems to get younger with every new government Bill, but if you're a woman and you live in Italy you can give birth as you collect your pension and if you're a man and only eat yoghurt and live in parts of Siberia you can procreate when a hundred-and-something. Of course there are, obviously, fixed dates in the almanac, and despite rocket science, it still takes four minutes to cook an egg. (The Indian law-giver Manu proclaimed, 14 centuries before the Christian era, that a woman 'would be adjudged an adulteress if she had been alone with a man the time it took to cook an egg'. Soft or hardboiled, would that be?) But, by and large, we can do what we want, when we want – and we'd like to keep it that way.

So I'd just like to know how it is that, when I enter a free-draw competition, in a country magazine which will remain nameless, I am required not only to give my name, address and telephone number but also my AGE? Since when was age a deciding factor for eligibility to win a pair of Swarowski *binoculars*, for heaven's sake?

I suppose you could say that if I'd put down that I was a 98-year-old male, the organisers might just have got a bit twitchy. ''Ere Joe, look at this then' they'd be saying in the office. 'Can't 'ave the likes of this geezer applying for free bins, up at dawn on the carncil estates takin' a peek, eh, probably on Viagra too dirty ol' bugger...' Well, *actually*, all I'm after is a decent pair of binos for stalking, for goodness' sake, as my family keeps pinching mine. And I'm fed up with having to make do with the old WW1 bridge-of-the-battleship numbers that no-one else wants either. Dawn sorties to stalk roe take on a whole new meaning when you have to be down at the back door by 2am to make sure some swine hasn't sneaked off with any of your gear. I suppose one could always sleep with all the stuff on, but you can imagine the problems – I mean, even the SAS don't share beds when they're fully kitted out.

We had a Belgian acquaintance to stay one year who was very keen on his roe. But he refused to get up at dawn to stalk and announced rather sniffily he'd only shoot *driven* roe, with a rifle, like he did at home. So we tried it. It was not, it has to be admitted, an unqualified success. Four of us lined out facing the end of a wood, the beaters were a bit apprehensive at first but there were lengthy instructions to everyone about absolutely not shooting in front, waiting until a beast had gone through the line before firing and so on.

The beaters all started walking up quietly from the other end of the wood, while we stood by our allotted bushes, some eighty-odd yards apart, and waited. Little birds flitted forward, a rabbit came out and washed his face – but no sign of a roe.

Suddenly there was shot from my left, where the Belgian was standing. I don't know what he had shot at, or in which direction he'd fired, but the woods echoed with the sound. This was immediately followed by a yell of 'That's it then boys', followed by the pounding of feet and crashing branches. Bit like a Goons sound-track really. It transpired that the beaters had decided that the Belgian wasn't safe and had, to a man, shinned up the nearest tree. (Infantry, of course. You can always tell an old infantryman: the cavalry can read maps, but for

37

sheer speed of footwork, the infantry have it every time.)

I don't know why I thought of this episode except that the Belgian was the first person I'd met who used Swarowksi glasses. Then there was a Norwegian who had a pair. He tried to persuade me to go on a trip with him shooting roe in Mongolia, saying I could then borrow his binoculars as well – a nice invitation but one which I had no hesitation in refusing especially once he'd informed me that, 'of course', we would be sharing a yurt. No of course about it. He had the physical appeal, and body-odour, of a yak, and a girl's got to hang on to her standards after all, even when it involves Swarowskis.

Swotting-up

For us girls here in the Big Smoke, there's good news. An exciting new men-only health club has opened in Mayfair, where your bloke can not only wind his heart-beat up to two-twenty on the exercise machines from hell, but can also get himself jaccuzied, body-waxed, pummelled, massaged, mani-cured, 'facially enhanced' and generally pampered and cossetted. He can spend several hours, or indeed a full day, swanning around soothed by sweet music and bikini-clad masseuses, drink-ing champagne or the latest version of green health-gloop, and swopping index prices with his chums whilst wearing nothing but a fresh white jumbo-sized fluffy, as it's known in the trade, about his firmly honed self. And looking exactly like an extra in *I, Claudius*. Woof woof. The price of a year's membership of this joint is, apparently, only marginally more than what I'm told you'd pay to take a party of eight onto a grouse moor.

Well. I mean, when you consider that the average English male thinks it's actually fairly wussy even to remove nasal hair, I can't see this as being a success of galactic magnitude, can you? Even in the capital. Older gentlemen of a certain age – the ex-House of Lords ilk, whose only exercise is on the corkscrew or the trigger-finger and who secretly yearn for the nursery and bread-and-butter pudding – surely won't be high on the waiting list. Nor, presumably, will the somewhat more prosaic hunter-gatherer type ('yeah-wewmait, 'morf to ve pub forra meaw, see?') Maybe it's more for the City boys, who push the sleeves of their Armani jackets well up above the wrist and drive Porsches. Or the New Man cosmopolitan types – skinny wife and beautiful kids, design-er loft in Docklands or large house in RBKC, plus Range Rover *and* 7-series in the underground garage.

Call me old-fashioned but I don't really trust men who work at the body-beautiful. It smacks of a Tadzio-like proclivity which really shouldn't be encouraged; *and* they're the ones who always notice if you've put on a pound or ten since last week... Give me the chunky outdoorsy type any day; the carefree, easy-going, Tom

Jones ones with a preppy smile and a healthy appetite who, when the wife (admittedly a blonde, and therefore possibly just a tiny bit flaky) announces 'Just nipping out to get a spot of dinner, ok?' automatically replies 'fine darling, take the Purdey'.

So, basically I like men who shoot, ok? Mind you, just because they do it doesn't necessarily mean they're good eggs... Difficult enough to tell in England, but I reckon if you stick to the ones with the very oldest, best-cut tweeds you won't go too far wrong. But go on a shoot abroad and you have even less of an idea of who's what. They don't even *wear* tweeds. It doesn't matter so much if you're actually shooting: but if you're not, you're then told by your other half: 'Go on, do your bit and stand with one of the other guns'. So, mentally running through your SWOT assessment list (Strengths, Weaknesses, Opportunities,Threats – does help being an army daughter) over the assembled line-up, you trot off obediently and take your chances as to whether he's the local duke or an axe-murderer.

It happened once on a shoot in Spain. I'd come out late with my hostess, just in time for the second drive, so had missed all the introduction bits, and was immediately and summarily despatched to be 'social' by the husband. 'And ...wat... outf... k...' he hissed at me indististinctly as, deaf to further injunctions, I obediently set off. There were the usual array of Spanish studs accompanied by feral women whom I by-passed, and continued down the line undeterred until arriving at a group of what looked like gorillas standing behind one fellow on his own, his *secretario* crouched down ready to load. Well, safety in numbers, I thought, so I marched up (he'd noticed and had very correctly stood up from his tripod seat and raised his hat), and stuck out my hand. 'Excuse me, we haven't been introduced but would you mind if I joined you for this drive?' I asked politely. 'O, and *buenos dias*, my name is Piffa'. The hat was nice and ancient, and he had that ole' preppy smile so I knew he wasn't an axe-murderer. 'Khow do you do' he said slowly, in softly-accented English. 'I am Juan. Hwat a plechure... Peeefa... hmmm... pliss sit...'

It was a great drive. Preppy shot fluidly and well, and talked happily non-stop throughout. The gorillas stayed strangely silent.

At the end of the drive, neighbouring guns came rushing up, bowing and blathering like maniacs. One of them then turned to me. 'Ees berry good esshot, ower keeng, eh?'

My mouth fell open like a postbox and Preppy started to laugh. 'I ham so sorry Peeefa,' he said kindly; 'but choo weel pliss choin me at lunch, no? We haff still many important tings to discuss I tink...'

Just how the hell was I supposed to know?

But the assessment list reads 'S<u>K</u>WOT' now. Just in case.

Don Miguel

D o you ever get the feeling that there's something wrong
with your eyes? Not that you're going blind of course but
a certain dimness there, a tad more bleariness than even
a smidgin of a hangover would warrant, a lack of focussing
power? *Anno Domini* probably accounts for a lot. I find that, after
working on papers for an hour or two, I then can't focus on anything further than 18 inches away. So I get up, walk out into the
street to get some fresh air and get run over. It's quite upsetting
really: statistics say that one person gets run over every hour and
I'm beginning to think it's me.

I've always worn glasses for driving and films – not bottle tops
mind you, they're only about .75 but they do make everything nice
and sharp and I can then also read price-tags out of the car window. Stalking in the rain isn't really a problem as you have a good
high-powered telescope, but scatter-gun shooting in a downpour
and glasses just isn't fun. Contact lenses are ok but, if you wear
them as I do for distant vision, you then can't focus on anything
close up. So a magnanimous gesture, say, at the shooting lunch
takes your plate with it and sends the wine all over the walls.
People then tend not to ask you out to smart restaurants much as
you're an environmental hazard.

On another occasion in Spain, when we had kindly been
asked to shoot some stags, I had my glasses with me as always

and, of course, binoculars. But there was a rather different problem here, also to do with 'distance', but this time it seemed to be the terrain that caused it. The *finca* we were staying in – a magnificent place with long marble corridors and hundreds of trophy heads along all the walls, stood at the centre of the property in the middle of a vast plain several miles wide, with tree-covered mountains rising up all around it. I had assumed that, as in Scotland, you would be taken to climb up into the hills and stalk your chosen beast, but no: every dawn and dusk, it seemed, you went out with the keeper, climbed no further than into a high seat, waited for something to wander down the mountain and venture out onto the bare plain, and shot it. Our host and old friend Miguel explained everything very clearly. 'Ees more essimple dis way, no? *Mira:* ju go aout, ees airly or ees after jur *siesta*, ju no get khot, de reelly beeg estag dey walk edown and *boum*, no? *Claro*, sometaime ees no so eesy but – *ehte* – for ju no problem ok?' and he puffed on one of the enormous Davidoff *puros* that he always kept clamped between his teeth, slapped me on the back and off we went, Domingo the *guardia* and I, dawn and dusk.

It was the position of the high-seat that was the poser, as it seemed to be a long way out from the edge of the mountains. And, although it's one thing to take a beast, if you have to, at 250 yards or so, it's quite another to be stuck half a mile or so away from it, out in the middle of nothing. But perhaps the stags came down through the trees, through the scrub at the bottom, and then meandered out onto the plain to eat... Eat what? Anyway Domigo was getting excited and nudging me as he twitched his binos. '*AhHA, señora,* looklook – *ahí esta uno*'. I couldn't see one anywhere. I scanned the mountains, the thick trees, the scrub – nothing. But after all, a brown stag, in the middle of brown scrub, at half-light, half a mile or so away, was never going to be exactly easy to see... If indeed it did come out and started walking, and then stopped to feed within shot, that would be great. But why would it walk that far out anyway? Domingo was getting more voluble... ok, something was there, something was moving all right, but still about six or seven hundred yards off... I could only barely make it out...

Domingo turned to me. '*Tíra lo*' he ordered. Shoot it? This wasn't Bisley for God's sake – I didn't have a cat's chance in hell of hitting anything, let alone hitting it correctly, at that distance. I shook my head. 'Not yet' I replied, 'it's too far'. The stag stopped, turned round, walked back into the scrub and disappeared into black trees. 'I'm sorry Domingo, it really was far too far away, I couldn't even see it properly through the 'scope...' He shook his head disgustedly. *'Ai de mi, señora, si tubiero sido Don Miguel, lo habra tirado'*. So that was that. If it had been Don Miguel, he'd have shot it.

This charade went on for three mornings and three evenings in succession. We sat in our high seat in the middle of the plain, we waited for hours, he saw stags, all I could see even through the 'scope were things that looked the size of hamsters, we waited for them to come out onto the plain, they didn't, he told me to shoot (400 yards, 600 yards, whatever), I wouldn't. And after each refusal came the accusing refrain *'Ai de mi, si tubiera sido Don Miguel...'* and we would walk home in silence. I was beginning to doubt my eyes, my judgement of distance, everything. Perhaps they had all been within shot after all? But then, I knew what a beast looked like at a shootable distance – or I thought I did.

That night, I accosted Miguel. 'Tell me, what rifle do you use for the stags off a high seat Miguel?' *'Ehte... vamos...* sisbyfif-teefour. Hwhy?' 'So, the same as the one I'm using?' *'Claro, queri-da,* ees my rifle ju hab.' 'And at what distance do you usually shoot a beast?'' Miguel slewed his *puro* round as he thought. *'Eh...* deeepens... twohunred metres, twofiftee – *mas o menos.'* 'So how come Domingo tells me to shoot stags at four hundred metres and more, and I always get this *Si-tubiera-sido-Don-Miguel* bit when I won't?'

He gave a shout of laughter. *'Ai...* dat man, always de beeg *exagerado...* He tink I am jenius, no? So he always tells de pipple I shoot longer dan dey. *Imbécil* – I talk to heem now, tomorrow ju will see, ju will get one estag, no problem.'

The following morning we went out and drove over the huge plain to a different high-seat some 300 yards out from the scrub. I watched the stag coming slowly down through the trees, walking out of the scrub, putting his head down to feed. It was a nice clean shot. Domingo was delighted. 'Good high-seat, that' I said non-commitally, as we dealt with the carcase. 'Don Miguel, does he use it much?' To give him credit, Domingo looked a trifle embarassed, then grinned broadly. '*Señora*, he always use dis seat. De odder, ees for shooting – howjusay *conejo*? *Si* – rabbit.'

Mars and Venus

———◆———

There are probably only three dates in the diary which are of any real significance to your average Englishman. The first is his birthday; next is December 25th, which he suddenly realises is Christmas Day and is, as usual, overcome by terror at the sight of wrapping paper and wishes he were in Timbuctu; the last is February 1st, the final day of the shooting season, the day on which grown males around the country spend the evening sobbing into the four-by-two and putting their shotguns to bed for the next 6 months.

Wonderful isn't it, how the two sexes differ... Who was the female aviator who announced proudly that 'there is no difference between men and women in the air'? Well, I can tell ya honey, that, although we're doing our level best down here, there sure is on *terra firma*. All that Mars and Venus stuff is for real. It's not just that men and women are obviously different; it's more that they are so *totally* different, with such amazingly differing priorities, desires and ideas; and what is fascinating to us women, some of whom take part, and are thus involved, in certain historically male-dominated areas of life, is just to what extent, and how. Male readers will cheer such visionary insight into the old male/female quandary. ''Bout time too I'd say' they'll snort; 'always maintained women shouldn't be meddling in Men's Affairs. Like clubs, or the MCC dammit, or the Forces, or field sports, or – well, hmm – things like that.' Right on, squire.

However, females are just as complete human beings, with minds as fine, and abilities as staggering, as men's and, although admittedly they have less physical strength, they have infinitely more intuition, imagination, concentration, guile and probably commonsense. I mean, a woman doesn't go all Schwarzenegger just because somebody cuts her up in the near lane; or deny 10,000 years of evolution, civilisation and philosophy by head-butting referees; or sulk when beaten at golf. I even know a man who actually shot the hinges off a fridge because the handle jammed. No, we're subtler than that. Any female can rub two boy scouts

together and make a fire you know; and she's just as capable of heading up the Stock Exchange or running MI5 as the next man. She can in fact do almost anything any man can do (apart from spending weeks in an AFV under battle conditions of course but I mean, who'd want to really – just think of the re-growth on your highlights for a start, plus a couple of other things which we won't go into right now).

Luckily nowadays this is no longer an issue, however alarming it may be for the old bulls running the once-male preserves. Sometimes though, it's the little things like buzz words that still trip some of us up. I confess I spent years thinking that 'silly mid-on' was just another term for the male menopause – so much for a convent education and no brothers. But today when the much-hyped 'glass ceiling' syndrome of the City has been splintered, any woman can now legitimately have a life, five children and good hair as well as flaunting the categorical imperative of killer-heels, flying jets, running Goldman Sachs, taking silk or a £3 million pay-cheque, talking knowledgeably about kick-boxing and take-overs and making comments like 'Hmm, market's pretty flaky right now' – all of which keeps the opposition in their baskets.

Men are of course always going to be miles better than we are at certain things. Apart from their obvious physical advantages, they can for instance calculate in three dimensions, which we can't and which makes them brilliant shots and superb drivers who understand the Oeteker Variant and total ace at ball-games, and endows them with the feel-good factor of macho superiority *and* automatic entry to the Playstation coterie where they can prove their prowess with BFG's (Big F***ing Guns – I do love all these acronyms don't you?). They also work extremely hard out of guilt, and once they are married, call their wives 'old thing'. And that's about it, really.

Whereas women enjoy the challenge of male enclaves, the converse is not necessarily true. Most men – English men at any rate – have neither the need nor the desire to understand the intricacies of the opposite sex. They like things to be basic, simple and straightforward, like joined-up meat: anything remotely esoteric – or, worse, romantic – is dismissed as being nancy. For instance, that incomprehensible female compulsion to straighten pictures, or discuss Hamlet, or rip out articles from newspapers or read novels (Real Men *never* read novels) or move furniture in the middle of the night, is they feel, merely deranged, like pelvic exercises. They don't understand it, it makes them feel excluded and therefore vulnerable and consequently ill-tempered.

The other thing that drives men mad is multi-tasking. (There are certain men who apparently still marvel that anyone can walk and chew gum at the same time.) This is, clearly, pre-eminently a female thing. Any moderately organised girl doesn't think twice about a morning routine that involves, for instance, hurtling into kitchen and opening post while squeezing healthjuice, checking watch against wall-clock and radio time-signals and checking data on lap-top and palm-held organiser; making appointments on mobile with relations, colleagues, girl-friends, tradesmen etc., also pre-orders for bike-couriers, next month's flights, vet, M.O.T and lobsters, whilst concurrently applying blow-torch to *crème brulée* for tonight's dinner, clicking onto e-mails and on-line banking, emptying dishwasher, writing lists, hoofing dead stuff out of brief-case and fridge, putting on lip-gloss, cheering up sick plant, checking mouse-bait and minutes of committee meeting, faking vinaigrette (out of bottle into pretty decanter), noting book reviews and fashion pages, sorting out share certificates and fabric samples and tax returns and collar-stiffeners *and* carrying on several perfectly logical discussions with mesmerised onlookers concerning last night's dreams, logistics of next weekend's travel plans, problem of juggling investment management with ok lifestyle plus relative merits of best friend's latest live-in, all at the same time, whilst also restraining over-enthusiastic retriever in Hapkido head-lock and waving around hands to admire rings and dry nail varnish.

The downside is that she'll probably then rush out moaning 'God I'm late' and slam the front door shut leaving the keys inside.

Well, we're not all perfect. But we're worth it.

Transports of Delight

Rather like Dr. Johnson, whose idea of pleasure was 'driving briskly in a post-chaise with a pretty women', I like my travel to be relaxed, easy... I hate all this hurtling through airports, ladened with Duty Free and emergency rations and the tool-kit for my face which weighs a ton, my Significant Other (who is the reason we're late, as always) pounding in front yelling blue murder at me ('Come ON, HURRY UP, WILL YOU GET A MOVE ON') while that world-weary voice booms over the loud-speaker 'Will the last two passengers on Flight Five-Oh-Niner come *immediately* to Gate 47 where the flight is now closing' and you know you're going to have apoplexy if you could only get your breath back to do so and you just want to lie down and sob.

Irate fellow travellers, lost luggage (how come it's always mine that ends up in Delhi? on a flight between Heathrow and *Glasgow* for God's sake?), toddlers throwing up into the fake plants and always, when you're sprinting flat out, a cleaning lady with one of those huge flat swingy mop things in the way... Airports suck. And of course it's that much worse when you're travelling with firearms as it takes half a day longer to check in and there's always a problem and everyone gets understandably twitchy when they find the odd cartridge in your shooting-jacket pocket as you push through the X-ray: 'JUST a moment madam, now WHAT have we here' and out come the rubber gloves and the queue behind starts muttering and getting restive... Once in the air things aren't necessarily that much better. One winter we had to take a small plane from Switzerland to get in to a tiny landing-strip in Austria for a shooting week-end. The winds were gale force, the pilot (he was only young, poor lamb, and it transpired much later that he'd only *just* qualified for his commercial licence) had never flown into that particular strip before. With any of these really hairy landing-strips, even when there's not a white-out and a storm and the mountains are within grabbing distance, the landing has to be *care*ful, like that old chestnut about hedgehogs making love. The little plane was bucketing up and down, I was too terrified to even think about being sick, the pilot was screaming in falsetto into the R.T. and was clearly not a happy bunny. I looked round (I'd been ordered to sit in the front seat: I have to tell you, it's murder in the front seat – you see all these little dials whizzing round like things possessed and the warning lights are flashing and that awful klaxon's yowling and you know you won't have a prayer when you do hit the wall as you're first in at the crash) and there was my husband, pale grey but *calm*, writing a codicil to his will on the back of a cheque-book. It was one of those rare moments when the expression 'anally retentive' had a lot going for it.

Old-fashioned methods of transport just have to be more relaxing. And you need relaxing, especially when you're going shooting as there's enough to worry about without wondering whether you'll be alive when you get there. Sashaying through long tiger-filled grasses on board an elephant, or navigating ice-floes on a sledge when you're after a bear in Alaska, or paddling through swamps after buffalo are quite taxing enough, what with the adrenaline and everything. Less hazardous to be sitting in a rickety farm cart spying Hungarian roe-deer, or even fending off an over-attentive Kurd or two atop a donkey, on your way to shoot mountain sheep... But the easiest and most comfortable mode of transport, and a pleasure of which Dr. Johnson would undoubtedly have approved, has to be when you're quail-shooting in Georgia, USA.

You sit in a mule-drawn carriage, knees covered in rugs against the early-morning chill, with two impeccably-liveried black coachmen chatting away to you the while and saying things like 'MAH, lawdy me, don't y'awl jus LURVE that Burdish ax-ent – say, yew awritee theya may'am ?'; and you trot smartly through tall pecan plantations, outriders abreast and the bells round the mules' necks clinking amicably, while pairs of hunting dogs scour the scrub to scent for birds and the day warms up nicely and there's a long table with barbecued quail and delicious iced wine for lunch in a shady clearing later on...

Mind you, y'awl are in Day-Glo hats and waistcoats so you don't shoot each other but, that apart, it's Vivien Leigh time. As a woman (and, moreover, a lady shot) you are cosseted and made to feel fragile and very special indeed, and you can wear smart leather boots and pretty tops and long leather skirts to shoot in (which you can't back home on account of the God-awful Burdish shooting weather with its mud and horizontal rain and the wire fences everywhere and the cholerous males who assume you're just vogue-ing anyway).

Here, if you do manage to connect with any of the minuscule feathered scuds exploding away through the bushes, the dog-handlers and the coachmen all whoop with joy. English shot-guns are considered something of an oddity, and a .20 bore side by side (with Monte Carlo stock) ellicits comments of a quaint ole southern nature. '*Wayal*, ah'll be furked where de sun doan shine – d'y'awl seen dat? But hey, dem lil burds dey jus wen straight to heaven... Dat was mydee fine may'am' – which is very good for a girl's morale in the shooting field.

Great place, Georgia.

Running Smoothly

———◆———

I dyed my Reebok trainers last week. 'You – *running shoes?*' an astonished girl-friend exclaimed; 'you, who thinks that the zenith of civilization as we know it means chauffeur-driven shopping and champagne in bed?' Yes, well, I don't actually *run* in them you know – my grandmother taught me that no lady *ever* runs – but they're awfully good for going for a brisk clip round the park and you can hose them down afterwards. And not having go-faster stripes doesn't make any difference as we're not into speed-mode here. Added to which, all that ergonomic sorbo and padded-gunk stuff makes you feel you're on Cloud 9. The only trouble was that they were brilliant white.

Now white of course is dead chic, and very IN this year, but if you've got feet the size of mine, wearing white trainers makes you look like something out of *The Clydesdale Heavy Horse Gazette*. So I dyed them brown. Well, that was the idea, but the leather dye didn't take terribly well on the sorbo, which then turned out the colour of undercooked mouse, but at least they now blend in nicely with whatever I tread in. Make no mistake, however, they are truly, deeply wonderful, and I merely pray I don't ever meet any of my tidier neighbours *en route* to the daily churn round the park...

All this unwonted heartiness stems from a deeply humiliating experience whilst shooting one arctic day last winter on the west coast of Scotland. I'd drawn the end peg which happened to be on the knoll of a small hill (and everyone knows that in the Scottish vernacular, the words 'yon wee hill' are used to denote any geo-physical feature of a protuberant nature whatsoever, up to and including K2) some 400 foot up, high above the shoreline where the rest of the guns were placed prior to addressing some serious pheasants and the odd woodcock which were programmed to come hurtling off the snowy tops with a gale behind them. That morning, I had carefully dressed for the arctic temperature and, wearing every single warm thing I possessed, bore an uncanny resemblance to a 50-tonner tyre. 'Just tak a pocket-fu and dinna

scorch yersel goin up' the keeper said kindly, as I set off. You
know that amazing sensation of being deafened as your heart
cannonades around your skull whilst simultaneously throttling
you to death? You think you're going to die, and then you're terrified you won't… It wasn't until I'd been overtaken half way up by
two fat sixteen-year-old labradors and a bunch of merry chatter-
ing children with flags, all going like smoke, plus the keeper's
seven-and-a-half months' pregnant wife who was leaping over the
heather to keep up with them while I lay tachycardic and sobbing
in a clump of scrub, that it finally hit me how totally unfit I was.

Hence the trainers. I'm not going to be shamed like that ever
again. Basically, I've always just been too lazy to exercise but
nowadays, as everyone gets more health-conscious, exercise is
almost *de rigeur*. Of course women have always been better at this
sort of masochism than men: it's been drummed into them
through decades of female lore that thin is beautiful and that love-
handles don't do anything for decent clothes, while men sneered
and said things like 'yeahwell, catch me doing any of that rubbish'
and grew bellies like Japanese pigs.

Not any more – oh no. Everyone's become health-conscious; and interestingly, it's even affected the shooting fraternity. For it's a fact that we've all become far too complacent about mollycoddling between drives and being driven to the butts; and shooting on fields as flat as stadiums with no fences to climb makes for wimps. 'Wouldn't have happened in m'father's day' one old boy waxed indignantly. 'Used to walk for miles as a young man – thought nothing of it. Eight hours after a stag, dance that night, every day for a month. Softies nowadays, the lot of 'em.' So now it's time to think positively: pound the pecs, go for the gluteus, firm the flab, discard the dross...

Which explains those over-weight, sagging corporate bodies doing American Air Force star-jumps and pulverising the bathroom floor and thrashing round the garden blowing like walruses and in a panic, having realised – too late – that the beguiling invitation to go stalking in Aberdeenshire, or shooting snipe in Kashmir, or sheep in Russia, or ptarmigan on some Godforsaken Munro, was proffered (and accepted) without a thought and several months ago, and they've now only got 4 days to lose 2 stone or else have a cardiac arrest on the hill which will look pretty stupid in the board's annual report.

Mind you, now that I've started, albeit very modestly, on this health-kick bit, it's amazing to find other self-conscious souls timidly emerging from the closet. A shooting friend actually admitted to having taken up running, doing the early-morning rounds of the West End daily before donning a stiff collar for meetings. I asked tentatively whether street-pounding wasn't awfully boring, even given the endorphines. 'Not at all' he replied, rather loftily. 'Just plan your route properly. Mine takes me past every known location of every single London gunsmith, past and present. Perfect couple of hours' run.'

As he's got abs like a bread-board, I worked it out later in the *A-Z* and reckoned the same route would probably take me a good two weeks to complete. But then he's probably got Reeboks with go-faster stripes.

Girl–Talk

———◆———

One of the flat-coats is just coming into season, the right moment to take her off to the nice lady breeder who has this really sexy good-looking dog standing by, with whom she (the flat-coat that is) will be able to indulge in a few days of unbridled lust and then return looking smug and thoroughly pleased with herself. It's always the same routine each time – lots of snaking and skittering about, and the most shameless flirting in an ooo-I-couldn't-possibly-what-*me*? manner; and then after-wards lying around with the paws crossed, looking at the nails as if butter wouldn't melt in the mouth and just a *teensy* bit tired, you know? *Enceinte* perhaps? Well...only by twenty minutes, but you've no *idea* how it tells on the legs... But that's girls for you.

A friend was telling me of the time he had taken his Labrador bitch up north to have her covered, travelling with her on the night sleeper to Edinburgh. At five o'clock in the morning when the train pulled in, one of the railway porters saw them both alighting and came up to gossip. 'Fine dog ye got there sorr' he said. 'They Labs, just toppers o' dogs ah reckon.' Delighted to find another canine enthusiast even at that early hour, Malcolm explained that the dog was, in fact, a bitch and he was taking her to the breeder to be mated. 'Wail, is tha' a farct?' replied the porter, bending down to ruffle the dog's ears in an affectionate fashion. 'So, yuz just up fer a durrrty weekend then are ye, pet?'

Females of certain species of flora and fauna come on heat in the most inconsiderate ways. Apparently in Moscow, female poplar trees do their bit for the reproductive cycle in May – for the whole month – which makes life fairly good torture for the local residents as there is poplar fluff flying about everywhere and getting into simply everything – into eyes and hair, up noses, into drinks and food, and probably into the brain too. The streets are carpeted in white as if it's been snowing with the stuff. The demand for anti-histamines brings every pharmacy to a standstill, and most intelligent Muscovites spend the month indoors with their windows hermetically sealed, communicating by phone whilst praying that these unsated arboreal Jezebels find what they're looking for, and fast.

I only mention this tedium in case anyone was mistakenly thinking of visiting Moscow in May or early June. But then why would anyone even contemplate leaving these shores at that time anyway – 'when the larks are singing and the dog-roses are in bloom' (the annual paean of a revered old Match Rifle shot, who would incant the same words every year at the final dinner of the June Cambridge Club Long Range Rifle Club meeting) and the chalk-streams and the roe-buck are at their best? The more you think about it, only a madman would go to Russia at that time. Except for the salmon fishing of course; but then you have to fight off mosquitoes the size of soup-plates which, as far as I'm concerned, makes it a no-no anyway.

Difficult problem, all this sex thing. No wonder country children grow up faster than townees: farmyard animals have absolutely no sense of discretion or of *pas devant les enfants*. 'OOOO mama, what's it DOING ?', and you really can't fudge it for ever. Explain everything, that's my theory; it may leave them boss-eyed, but it saves a lot of trouble later on. Unlike that famous story of Noel Coward at Brighton, who, on being asked by a small boy what two dogs were doing on the sea-front, replied: 'Well, the dog in front is blind, and the one behind is very kindly pushing it all the way to St. Dunstan's.'

Whilst we're on the subject of dogs and sex and things (I'm sorry, none of this has anything at all to do with shooting, but you can't win 'em all), a very dear friend, the Past President of the Royal Society of Portrait Painters, told me about a conversation he'd once had with a particular client – the now long-dead Bishop of Christchurch, New Zealand – whose portrait he was then engaged on. The eminent Bishop turned out, much to George's relief and delight, to be a particularly garrulous and therefore easy subject – (it's often quite tricky for the portrait painter, as he has to ensure that he keeps his subject looking animated and doesn't allow him to fall asleep) and conversation was rollicking on happily. In the general flow of chat, the Bishop started to talk about women, and asked George whether it was difficult to paint them because of their – um – SHAPE ? George replied no, you just painted what you saw. 'Ah-ha' answered the Bishop. 'Then that depends on the type of *braz-year* they're wearing doesn't it' and went on to explain that, to the uninitiated such as himself, there were apparently three types of 'braz-years': there was 'the Salvation Army model, for the uplift of the masses; the Soviet Army model, for the suppression of the masses; and the US Atomic model, for 90% fallout.'

Several years later, George was painting the portrait of the then Professor of Anatomy of a famous English university Medical School. During the course of the sittings, talk turned somewhat naturally to the subject of anatomy, and George recounted what the Bishop had told him. There was a pause. 'Ah yes' dreamily replied the Professor, 'but I think I know a more local version – the sheepdog model; it rounds them up and points them in the right direction, hmmm?'

Obviously a country-man at heart.

Keep Your Hair On

G oing down to shoot in the West Country; and instead of a six-hour slog on the motorway the train seems a more civilised option. I love travelling by rail – 'let the train take the strain' and all that... The romance of early rail-travel was undeniable; think of those two marvellous George Earl paintings of the early 1890s, *Going North* and *Coming South*: the porters, the men in long caped coats and the women with large hats; the ghillies and the dogs and the shooting cases; and children haring about; and fur rugs and panniers and sporting equipment and fishing gear and travelling trunks everywhere; all the paraphernalia and glamour of holidays, spilling over in the general hectic chaos of stations alive with the excitement of a journey, going north from King's Cross in the late summer, or returning south from Perth, with the trophies and the dead game... It must have been wonderful.

Nowadays of course, wonderful it ain't – and certainly not in that sense of style and excitement. And there are too many horror stories to make any of the BR/PR hype totally credible. But if you should, despite such understandable misgivings, decide to travel by train, and you are on your way to a shoot, take a tip from one who knows: never *bring* what is obviously a shotgun case on board, as you're then greeted by the sideways glances and hissing and snarling from other passengers with their polystyrene coffee-cups and their newspapers and their haversacks and their laptops and their city suits and their WI pearls...

One woman actually *spat* at me in a carriage, having watched me struggling on with a cartridge bag and a shotgun case as well as a suitcase, wearing boots and what was obviously shooting jacket and a hat with duck-bottoms on it... Not again. Nowadays I break my gun and pack it, together with an empty cartridge bag and the gun-slip, and the two-piece cleaning rod and the boots and the shooting jacket, in the suitcase, and pray there will be a nice strong porter at the other end and that my host hasn't forgotten that I've got to buy ammunition off him. And I don't wear a hat with feathers in.

Talk about the Liberty to Choose – why are we made to feel so guilty? One cold wet winter's day in London my daughter and the dog, having hailed a taxi (the two of them were having a girls' day together – you know, having the hair done, spot of lunch, manicure etc.) the daughter then asked the cabbie, very properly, if he would mind having a dog on board and got the reply 'No, but I do mind young ladies wearing fur'. She then had to stand in the rain arguing, before finally swearing it was fake. Which it was, as a matter of fact – but that wasn't the point.

On the other hand some people are, luckily, more tolerant. I once took the photograph of a superb wild goat I had shot – it was very beautiful and of an unusual colour, with lots of varying shades of beige and blonde and with extremely good platinum stripes on top – into the hairdresser with the request that he copy the colours onto my hair. Everyone fell about at that, but he very nicely said that it made an interesting change from the pictures of models and film stars that were normally brought in, and did a brilliant job. (In case there are any men out there still living in the dark ages, statistics show that at least 60% of women colour their hair nowadays – and some men too I'll be bound.)

Whilst we're on the subject of hair, I do remember an awful occasion out shooting, when a man several pegs down the line lost his hat in the wind, and his hairpiece went with it. It was, to be fair, the most singularly ill-made contraption which had fooled no-one and which made him look as if he was wearing a dead cat on his head but he was, somewhat understandably, totally mortified. Matters were then made worse when the offending *toupée* went bowling off along the ground and his neighbour took a shot at it, claiming afterwards that he meant no offence and had simply thought it was a runner...

Of course it must be difficult for men, who never want to admit they're going bald anyway, and so indulge in that sad farce of raking some strange and suspiciously *gommina*'d long bits over the bare pate, and then having to watch out for the wind lest they get caught amidships and end up looking like Woodstock in a gale. Who ever do they think they're fooling? Better by far to submit cheerfully, I reckon – have your head polished and buffed once a week by a decent barber who has one of those nice old-fashioned roller things – as in a car-wash – suspended from the ceiling; and wear a good fur hat in winter...

Girls, especially in the shooting field, can have a tricky time with anything other than very short – or very long – hair; but then they can either wear a suitable shooting hat (preferably something chic but not bizarre) or else just put up with looking less than totally perfect during the morning, and remember to bring the heated tongs in the handbag for a quick make-over before lunch. Style, in the shooting field, has to do with your gun-mounting not your coiffure. Which is something of a comfort after all, even for the vainest amongst us.

Poetic Licence

O ne day last season, my shotgun went dead. Nothing shattering or dramatic, just no trigger-pull – nothing. Stupidly, I accepted someone's generous offer of 'Oh don't worry, I'll send it off for you to my little man, he'll fix it in a tick, ready for you next week, ok?' Next week, my little gun duly came back. I fired two shots with it and that was it – dead again, and this time with a peculiar, and very distinctive, sound of little thingummies or small aliens rattling about inside.

I then did what I should of course have done originally and sent the gun off to its maker, together with a note explaining what had happened. I do this anyway once a year, when it returns happy and purring and looking well after an MOT with Mother. This time, Mother had attached a little note with a tiny piece of metal taped to it. 'Dear Piffa, I enclose part of the left firing pin which was found inside your gun. Most unusually, the back of the pin had broken, something I have not seen in my 25 years with this firm...' The moral is obvious: like face-lifts or daughters, your guns should never, *ever*, be mucked about with by anyone else's 'little man'.

I do confess that, along with the solar and the digestive systems, the inner workings of the internal combustion engine, or indeed whatever little daily miracles take place in an egg, or a brain or under the bonnet of my car, I find the inner workings of a firearm are mysterious, wonderful and totally incomprehensible. Not that it gives me sleepless nights, mind you: like cars, I don't need to know what makes them work; I'm a moron, I just drive them. (I don't fettle my own rifle ammunition either.) So to have been taken round a traditional English Gunmaker's factory recently, and to have been shown exactly how every single piece of wood that is used, and every single one of those myriads of small metal pieces, is not only whittled by hand, but is *signed by the whittler*, is a seriously impressive experience.

It also makes one realize exactly why a

bespoke pair of English shotguns, made by one of these Great English Gunmakers, can and does cost rather more than the GNP of most small countries. Anyone who owned or had ever owned a shotgun or a rifle, no matter by whom it was built, would have given their little ears to have been taken on such a tour. And, because I happened to be re-reading him for the umpteenth time, I wondered whether Henry Reed, author of that wonderful poem *Lessons of the War* (the first 5 stanzas, *Naming of Parts*, are the famous ones, and deal with all the parts of a rifle; the following 7 stanzas are called *Judging Distances*) had ever been taken round a gunmaker's factory, although I rather imagine not.

As a war-poet, Reed is, sadly, probably remembered only for that one piece. Regardless of its merits as a fine, delicate, humorous and very evocative piece of writing, for anyone who has ever suffered the humiliating attentions of a Weapons Instructor (' 'Ere we 'ave, gennelmen, the perfkt hexample of 'ow *not* to strip a Bren gun in firty seconds, *do* Oi make myself clear?') – or indeed has ever fired, and then cleaned, a rifle at all – *Naming of Parts* is without any doubt required reading. As Match Rifle shots, we used to incant it, like a grace before dinner, and also, when in Scotland, before addressing the glen target at the sillier distances of over a mile. It just seemed the thing to do. '*Today...*' someone would start off in lugubrious tones, and everybody else would join in, '*Today, we have naming of parts. Yesterday, / We had daily cleaning. And tomorrow morning / We shall have what to do after firing. But today, / Today we have naming of parts...*'

Unsurprisingly I suppose, poems about shooting are fairly rare. Certainly the great English Nature Poets weren't any help at all, being much more interested, for their own obscure reasons, in daffodils, or Odes to Autumn, than in writing a decent piece of verse about waiting for duck at sunset, or roe-stalking at dawn. Virgil, on the other hand, was a Good Thing and must surely be the hero of all doughty shooting men – '*Arma virumque cano*' and so forth... Our modern poets aren't generally so *muscular* are they? Mind you, try starting off the first line of your own slim volume with the words 'I sing of arms and the man': the resulting publication might well find itself relegated (thanks to the one-watt initiative of some female temp who hasn't had the benefit of a classical education), together with other questionable and mostly Hard Core stuff, onto the topmost shelf of the Adult section. Or, indeed, incite a visit by the local fuzz.

Interesting what the fuzz get exercised about these days. You can understand their concern in matters to do with firearms of course (although in years gone by the cunning shoot-owner always included the local Chief Constable as one of the guns on a really good January day at the long-tails...) However I was told a rather surprising tale by some people who'd asked a French friend over to England, to stay for a weekend house-party which included a day's shooting on the Saturday. The shoot included some very good drives, especially a really productive one called The Hanging – a very common name for wooded hilly areas in the south of England, and which refers to the old sites of the mediae-val woods which did indeed 'hang' above the valleys in that part of the country.

On his return home, the well-mannered Frenchman immedi-ately, and very correctly, telephoned the European version of Interflora and ordered a small card to be sent, pinned to a large bunch of flowers, to his English hostess. The message on the card had been duly and carefully written out in capitals following his instructions, and read: 'THANK YOU FOR THE WEEKEND AND ALL THE WONDERFUL ENTERTAINMENT. THE HANGING WAS VERY AMUSING. MILLE MERCIS.'

The florist apparently panicked, and Interpol was on to his hosts like a flash.

A Monumental Boar

———◆———

We were going to shoot boar in Belgium. Wonderful invitation, driven boar – exciting with a hint of danger – heart-racing business. You stand, up to twenty guns, round a vast area of forest facing in to the drive, where scores of beaters with assorted dogs march in line, blowing horns, shouting and yelling, the dogs yelping and barking like maniacs. Every so often a boar – or a sow followed by a scurrying line of her piglets, their tails held straight up like antennae – escapes from the pursuers through the line of guns: you may shoot only once the boar has crossed the line (it's quite important to remember this, otherwise you're shooting towards the beaters who tend to get excitable or go on strike if that happens, so basically it's discouraged). At the end of the day there is the *tableau de chasse,* lines of dead beasts laid out in rows while the hunting horns are played, which is a wonderful sound and very goose-bumpy, while the tall flaming torches splutter and flare in the gathering dark... *La Vénerie* is a thrilling and deeply romantic sport, famously chronicled by Gaston Phoebus, the Comte de Foix, in the early 13th century, when it was done from horseback and with packs of boarhounds, in his great tome, *Le Livre de Chasse.*

The only thing is, you want to make sure you do it right. In all spheres of life, there is a traditional, or accepted, way of doing things; for instance when shooting boar, there is the recognized format of words with which you accept the '*Weidmannsheil*', the formal traditional greeting and honour given to you once you have shot a beast; a small matter, but the etiquette has to be properly and correctly observed. But as to the actual shooting of a beast, you want to get that right too; and not just for reasons of 'manners' either, but for a far more basic motive: you are hunting something that can bite back, and if you get it wrong it can really sting. I know I'm a wimp but luckily, being a woman, I don't have to prove anything to the contrary: all that macho stuff of wounded buffalo or bear-wrestling – not for me, honeybun. I'm not fourteen foot tall and bullet-proof and I just hate being frightened. I don't even go into a farmyard where there are *geese* for heaven's sake...

But I digress. Here we were on a lovely cold, crisp day in November, in the Ardennes. After a huge breakfast of coffee and schnapps, cured meats, 15 different types of cheese and *pain au chocolat*, there was an hour's easy drive through wild countryside and the early morning mist to join the rest of the party at the meeting place, an old hunting lodge on the edge of the forest. It could have been the Middle Ages: fires burned brightly in braziers, goblets of wine were handed round, the uniformed *guardiens de chasse* and some thirty or more hunters and friends milled about, there were shouts of laughter and a huge amount of excited talk...you can picture the scene.

A boar-hunt in Belgium is a frightfully smart affair. There's bound to be an uncrowned royal in the party, plus a brace of dukes and the odd vicomte – Eurocrats all, wearing proper high leather boots and with shaving brushes in their hats. Women – women always come out to watch – are in full-length fur coats crying *'ah que c'est gai'* to other women and smoking Balkan Sobranies and flirting ostentatiously with the dukes. I felt foolish in my Scottish shooting tweeds. A good-looking man in a double-caped loden with old crested silver buttons on came up to me and, bowing, swept off his hat. *'Bonjour madame*, aa unnerstan yew are shooteeng toodey, *mes compliments...* ye ave dun ziz menny taimes beefur, yuz?' Feeling about six I said no, well, erm, actually

I'd never shot boar before and thought it might be a tad tricky, so I'd probably just have to watch him, I mean everyone, ha ha, for a bit, just to get the hang of it. 'Bert' he said kindly, 'eet ees verey eeesi – all yew ave to do ees tek zem laike reybets, *boum-boum* laike zat, as zey go pest. Ennywey, aa weesh yew lurk' and swept off. A duke, unquestionably, but not much help.

After the first drive I understood exactly what the problem was going to be. That '*boum-boum*' thing was the key to it. They all had chic little double-barrelled rifles, and swung easily on the beast as it crashed out of the undergrowth and thundered past, crossing the ride where it either got shot or disappeared into the forest behind, pursued by a pack of hounds from hell. But I didn't have a chic little double-barrelled rifle. What I had was my nice old stalking rifle with the welded-on telescope sight. This is not the way to shoot driven game 'laike reybets' as, instead of swinging the rifle like a shotgun, and trying to look over or under the 'scope with both eyes open, what I'd tried to do at first was focus the 'scope onto the moving target; and of course that way, however much you screw down the magnification, you don't have a snowflake's chance of hitting something hurtling past at 60 miles an hour about fifteen feet away. It was a nightmare, and all I was managing to do was bring down the odd sapling.

You can't afford to make a mistake, either, as if you merely wing the thing it won't think it at all *gai* (they get quite cross, boar) and can well turn and come back at you -150 kilos, no sense of humour and going at speed. And in Belgian forests, the trees are manicured pine with no lower branches to leap into. Added to which I got the impression that it would be decidedly *mal-vu* to be found, swinging and gibbering in mid-air like some demented tweed-swathed baboon. The dukes would raise an eyebrow.

Three drives later I reckoned I'd cracked it. Waiting until a boar had rushed past me across the ride, tail up and making off into the woods behind where you could shoot, luckily with no dogs in tow (he was absolutely huge, I don't know why they hadn't cottoned on to him) I held fire until he was about 60 yards out, going away clearly and in a straight line, and perfectly in focus through the scope; then, using what might be termed the most *natural* of aiming marks, got him spot on.

The *guardien* seemed a trifle non-plussed afterwards, as he couldn't find the bullet's point of entry; and I certainly wasn't going to tell him since – although an impeccably safe and undeniably sporting shot – I felt it might not conform to the pure and rigourous standards of *La Vénerie*.

But I did own up later to my host and, luckily, it afforded general amusement being, apparently, a most unusual feat of marksmanship.

Bargain Hunting

It's strange to think that, although the earth has been in existence (according to those pre-Cambrian proterozoic experts) for over 500 billion years, and human life culture for some 14 million years, some of us – well, one of us anyway – still hasn't yet worked out one of the basic principles of life, namely, there's no such thing as a bargain. I'm a total sucker for bargains. Pathetic really: trawling through boot sales, auction houses, junk-shops and antique emporia the length and breadth of the country, spending a fortune on petrol, train fares and shoe-leather, hunting and haggling for the ultimate *trouvaille*... Once I drove three hours north to look at some supposedly 'Chippendale' chairs which I'd seen advertised as going for a song. When a fine original Chippendale carver can sell at auction for a king's ransom, what in God's name would make anyone with even half a brain cell imagine that one costing 40 quid was going to be a must-have? The chairs were heavily dyed a startling pitch-black, with legs like knobkerries, and had clearly been hacked out of local timber by a fairly inventive gorilla with a bit of spare time up a tree in some rain forest... It was quite funny really. But to a bargain-addict, the mere possibility was irresistible, of course. I happily drove home empty-handed, only pausing at the filling station to congratulate myself on impeccable judgement... Such intelligence.

It's the squirrel genes that gets us all. There can't be a living soul who at one time or another hasn't started collecting, usually at school with stamps or conkers, and some never lose the urge for the rest of their lives. My old university tutor confided that, as a boy, he had started collecting moths. One day, meandering round his parents' library, he managed to heave down a large tome off a shelf and seeing the title, realized, to his huge excitement, that he'd discovered what was obviously a reference book on precisely his favourite subject – a lepidopterist's manual for children. The book

(entitled *Advice To Young Mothers*) turned out of course to be nothing of the sort. The experience so shattered him that he thenceforth turned to collecting football cards, which seemed altogether safer and which admitted no ambiguities whatsoever.

A little while ago a shooting friend and I went to one of the viewing days of an Arms and Militaria auction. It was going to be a big sale – 600-odd lots of modern and antique guns and 'related items'. I made straight for the 'related' section. There were stock blanks and apprentices' engraving plates, turnscrews and nipple keys (which did sound painful, but one had a whistle attached which must have been handy); uniforms, boots and helmets and bugles; edged weapons, powder flasks, blanks for stocks and cannon breech-brushes, and the job-lots of paper cartridges, antique tools and old horn oil bottles. There were lovely old leather guncases full of mouse-droppings and cartridge magazines, there were clamps and crimpers and re-loading tools. And there were books by the ton, and old prints and makers' labels by the score. I was in heaven.

My friend (an erstwhile general) strolled off meanwhile to look for a decent stalking rifle amongst the hundreds of lots on offer. You could examine and play with every one to your heart's content: percussion, flintlock and obsolete firearms; service rifles, match rifles and hammer-guns; punt-guns and muskets, revolvers, blunderbuss and 'overcoat' pistols; and a pair of 19th century highly decorated Turkish flintlock holster pistols, with silver plates on the stocks (engraved with dogs, birds and flowers) as well as shotguns and sporting rifles of every age, description and condition – big bores, small bores, single, double and triple-barrelled.

After about an hour he appeared, bearing something in triumph. 'It's a Mauser, practically unused, with a .243 barrel and a Zeiss 'scope, and I've got some old ammo for that. But look, it's also got – and this is the fun part – an *interchangeable .270 barrel*, which is the calibre I really wanted, and also with a Zeiss… wonder if it's worth it…?' A small friendly crowd – gunmakers and dealers all – gathered round immediately like Santa's little helpers, interested to see, help and comment. 'Yeah, an' it's in ok nick, innit? …' 'Fair estimate – reckon it's a bargain, two rifles for the price of one, the 'scopes alone are worth that …' '…and think, being able to change barrels at whim, just like changing chokes eh?...'

Apart from the question of why you'd ever want to change barrels whilst actually out in the field – unless you were suddenly attacked by lions of course – it did seem brilliant. Then I had thought. 'I know this sounds silly but, if you *are* meant to be able to just switch-and-go, without totally dismantling the rifle, um... how do you actually *do* it?' I asked. They all smiled nicely (typical dumb female question) and had some fun. 'Dunno, but it's gotta be a doddle...' 'Get someone else...' 'S'right, probably just throw your leg over it and Bob's your proverbial...' The general grinned. 'Well,' he said cheerfully, 'help definitely needed here, as I certainly haven't a clue: anyone know how this "quick-change" thing works...?' As one, twenty heads craned over the rifle on the table, its extra barrel lying tantalisingly orphaned by its side, and for a moment there was silence.

'Perhaps...' someone suggested tentatively, 'that lever there...' and then it was Babel: shouts of laughter and talk, arguing, ribbing each other, all full of enthusiasm, eager to help a newcomer in his moment of need. They poked and peered and prodded and passed the rifle from hand to hand, searching for clues; they discussed catches and flanges and male screws and female apertures and lengths and corresponding attachments and receivers and protuberances and allen keys and piling swivels and how – come on guys – all you had to do, *surely*, was take the barrel like *so* and twist it like so in one fluid movement (after all the catalogue did specify 'quick-release', didn't it – or was that the 'scopes...) and it all sounded very *Boy's Own* and deeply impressive. Absolutely nothing happened. The barrel glinted nastily and didn't budge.

After 15 minutes of this I caught the general's eye and we both started to giggle; it was just ludicrous: all the experts in the land, suffering barrel-baffle... Those around us saw the joke, gradually the rest of the room joined in, and suddenly everyone was laughing helplessly, in sheer disbelief at the idiocy of the situation.

Before he left, after being shaken warmly by the hand by the whole assembly, the general, urged on by his new best friends, left an insultingly low bid on the thing. He got it. I only hope he can learn how to change barrels before the lions appear.

Speed, Direction, Angle

Walking back to the pavilion after a particularly depressing lesson in the grouse lay-outs, I fell into conversation with someone who is a very well-known game shot and a shoot owner, but who also competes at clay targets and Olympic shotgun disciplines. One of those people who make it all look so easy that you feel you'd do better to stick to macramé; and I was yarping on about how hard I found it to make good shots consistently, and how I really had to *think* about what to do each time, instead of doing it just by reflex. He listened seriously, paused and then delivered the *coup de grace*. 'Well um… of course the more you THINK about a shot, the slimmer your chances are, as you'll start to aim rather than swing. But that apart, it is also a commonly-known fact that there's a part of the brain that deals with 3-dimensional or spatial logic, and females don't have it.'

Oh? Really? Commonly-known by WHOM, pray? 'Brain surgeons actually. Nothing to do with brain-power of course' he went on quickly. 'It's just that the male brain can immediately grasp the spatial concept of direction, speed and angle, whereas the female brain only 'sees' two of those things and then has to work out the third. Only takes a split second, of course, but that's when you miss the shot.' He laughed, kindly. 'Well, that's the theory anyway.'

So – I'm spatially dyslexic. Great. 'So you're saying that even the very best woman shot will never be as good as the best man?' 'Exactly; and that's why there are different classes for men and women for clay-shooting at competition level. And also, if you take it further, why there's never been a Formula One female driver; and why women can't catch cricket balls. Same problem, you see – speed, direction and angle. However as far as *working* at a problem goes, women are far more dedicated than men, so you'll probably get there and beat us all in the end.'

And here I've been, wittering on for aeons about how a woman can be equally as good a shot as any man, only to be told that my neurons aren't up to it. Part of the gender battle yet again? (Like the old joke 'Don't question your wife's judgement, look who she married'.) You simply cannot go round telling a woman she's neurologically challenged, it's like telling a man his equipment isn't all it could be. Mind you, I know men who aren't all that good at putting two, let alone three, dimensions together; all fine and dandy when it's blondes on laps at Stringfellows, agreed – but try getting them to put a ticket the right way up into one of those nifty little machines in the Underground, whilst keeping the queue, building up behind, out of lynch mode, and hey presto – the ole' direction-speed-angle theory's up the spout – just can't hack it.

But enough of these cheap gibes. Maybe, just maybe, there was something in what he'd said? I reckoned I could usually get 2 out of the 3 variables, but then the third (and it wasn't always the same one) always eluded me. So you worked on that one, and once you'd got it, one of the others took off. Exactly like trying to pin down mercury or catch hens. And of course, that bit about 'thinking' about a shot was absolutely right, and explains that very irritating phenomenon of only ever being able to bring down a bird I've not had time to think about – whereas those nice easy shots, straight overhead with all the time in the world – forget it...

Now I understand why men never seem to suffer any such problems. Men can, and do, just shoot well 'naturally'. They are aggressive by nature; women aren't. The term 'aggressive woman' is an oxymoron, like 'military intelligence'; and you can no more expect a woman to be naturally aggressive than you can expect a man to knit a G-spot. Men never need to analyse a shot, they just do it. Hence those infuriating remarks like 'I dunno – just put the gun up and shoot, dammit – stop thinking about it all – be positive; step into the shot then up and bang, just like that.' That after all was the attitude of their forefathers, who'd had their guns built for them in the year dot, when the only bit of analysis they'd ever made was 'full choke for the right barrel, quarter in the left' – so you got the first incomer well in front and the second one wasn't shot to pieces and plucked and oven-ready by the time it hit the ground. This would have been, of course, only for shooting on a grouse moor. *Gentlemen* only ever shot grouse: 'pheasants are for peasants' was the old rather dismissive dictum of the early 1900s.

Times change, however, and as a child in Ireland I well remember one of my grandfather's cronies coming out to shoot with us on pheasant days – a splendid, very crippled, very deaf and very ancient general who was also an extremely fine shot.

The ritual of his shooting day never altered by one iota. He was always driven right up to his peg by a fearsome Irish ex-batman who, as well as being his chauffeur, was also butler, loader, nanny and factotum. Apart from the usual impedimenta – shotguns, shooting stick, cartridge bag and fine leather gloves – the butler always produced a small suede bag and a large tin of strong peppermints. Having settled himself onto his shooting stick with all the precision of a nesting vulture, the general would remove his false teeth and place them in the small suede bag, and would then choose a peppermint on which to suck. Once this had been accomplished, the butler would load one of the guns, hand it to the general, and stand immediately and silently behind him.

As a bird approached, the general – who may have been as old as Methuselah but had absolutely nothing wrong with his eyesight – would stagger to his feet and, with a loud rallying-cry of 'Steady the Buffs now Hyssop' (the butler had been an altar-boy in his youth, heaven knows what his real name was, everyone addressed him as that) would fire, well out in front, Hyssop holding him up for the shot.

Up and bang, just like that. Between them, they never missed a bird.

All Fired Up

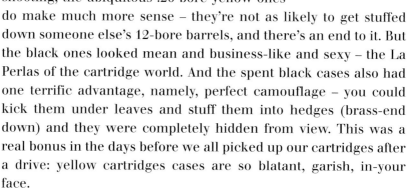

I do regret the demise of the old black Rottweil .20 bore cartridges. Of course, for safety reasons, which are the only seriously good reasons for anything out shooting, the ubiquitous .20 bore yellow ones do make much more sense – they're not as likely to get stuffed down someone else's 12-bore barrels, and there's an end to it. But the black ones looked mean and business-like and sexy – the La Perlas of the cartridge world. And the spent black cases also had one terrific advantage, namely, perfect camouflage – you could kick them under leaves and stuff them into hedges (brass-end down) and they were completely hidden from view. This was a real bonus in the days before we all picked up our cartridges after a drive: yellow cartridges cases are so blatant, garish, in-your face.

Most shooting men won't understand any of this but any novice lady shooting a .20 bore will know exactly what I mean. It's been a really stupendous drive with masses of truly great birds. And there, littered about your feet like the manic remains of some wild Hungarian orgy are hundreds of these bright little sunshine-coloured cases all screaming 'BOYwasthatFUN'. Which is all very jolly except for the fact that you didn't manage to hit a thing, and you just wish to God the earth would open up and swallow you. 'Ahhh good, you HAVE been busy, let's see...' says your host in a satisfied tone as he comes down the line at the end of the drive; 'don't move, we'll get a dog for you...' And you shuffle miserably from foot to foot muttering 'Well... EKTually... erm...' and praying that you, or he, will encounter some other small distraction – a bolt from heaven would be nice – anything to prevent him count-ing up the garish testimonials of your ineptitude. (No lady should ever admit to not shooting straight. Of course no gentleman would ever ask her – 'straight out, just like that, bloody rude' as the limerick goes. Phrases like 'Heavens what a drive – truly amazing' or, better still 'They were far too good for me I'm afraid' can get you out of too much trouble, both absolving you from being deemed a total cretin and complimenting your host at the same time. With any luck, it will also placate him well enough to keep your name on any future guest list.)

It's odd that, although for the unimpeachable reason above, .20 bore cartridges now have to be yellow and .16 bore ones have to be blue, there seems to be no hard and fast rule for .12 bore cases. I suppose on the grounds that there are more .12 bore cartridges sold generally, their cases have now become a sort of advertising medium and thus it is generally-accepted that any colour, other than yellow or blue, may be used on a .12 bore case.

So that's that. It's actually not worth thinking about cartridges much further. Suffice to say that there is almost nothing more boring – except perhaps watching Morris dancing – than those interminable conversations you get to hear between two men, each intent on impressing the other with their own breed of squibs. 'Mmm, yers... well I suppose if you find they really suit you, well and good. But I now get mine specially built for me of course, eleven-fifty p.s., and extra brass makes all the difference I find... Rather good design on the cases too I think you'll agree? – that way I can tell if anyone's swiped some huh huh.' Turned out they were in his racing colours. What a wally.

It's just like those men who go on and on and ON to one another about cars – multi-eject and 10-inch pipes and better responses over two-fifty and all that Thrust/SSC garbage. We all know it's just basically shorthand for 'I've got a bigger one than you mate', but how come all this Top Gear stuff is invariably spewed out by men who have all the sex-appeal of a Robin Reliant? I can't think of a single woman who has ever been impressed by it either. It's much more fun watching an Italian waiter demonstrating a pepper-mill.

On the other hand, I do understand the marketing boys' viewpoint: surely anything that looks flash and has a name like Ultimate Express or Sooper Dooper High Bird or FU2 or Banged Up ('yeah yeah, vat's very good') must sell better to the average customer? You can just imagine them at the Creative Input meetings can't you. 'Now come ON team, gotta think of a design and a name for these little beauts, something that'll really get the punter fired up ha ha ha, no ducky it's a joke – Oh for heaven's sake – anyway, over to you Tristram, this is just up your street sweetie' and Tristram (not a shooting man himself but who *reeelly* fancies young Maud – his name's Montgomery but they all call him Maud – over at the factory and they discuss powder and things together) mouths 'thooper' and blows him a kiss and goes off for a two-week company-paid Deep Thought Break in the Caymans before faxing back to H.Q.: 'Hows about faux-fur-print case with a hint of steel called Doberman Gotcha' and getting a bonus. Bet it wasn't like that in the old Eley days.

It's a bit like the Cresta really: the smart-ass wannabe does it clad in go-faster stripes and expensive lycra to reduce wind-resistance, the gentleman amateur does it in his pa's old tweed breeks and still believes that, like money, wind shouldn't be mentioned. Doesn't stop either of them coming out at Shuttlecock of course, it's just a matter of New style v. Old.

I saw some really nasty new .12 bore cartridges a while ago – see-through, they were, most unappealing, like condoms for aardvarks. No wonder we're encouraged to pick up our empties, you can imagine what the local children might make of the goings-on in the shooting field if they discovered things like that in a hedge. But as everyone except the Tristrams of this world know, it doesn't matter a hoot what a cartridge is called, or indeed what colour it is, *so long as* it's the correct size for your gun and it's let off in the right direction. Certainly, for the professionals and the CPSA shots there is more to it than this; but for your aver-age shotgun enthusiast, who isn't going to screw in different chokes every eight minutes, or worry overly about the p.s. factor, but is just going pottering about the hedgerows with a dog or hav-ing a good day out with friends, a pocketful of just about anything is fine.

So why ever have I been banging on about it... There are only two rules for shooting: be safe, and mind your eye. Or as Sir Henry Halford, court physician to George III, George IV, William IV and Queen Victoria, said, when asked to give his recommendations for the Maintenance of Health: 'Never drink claret in an east wind; and never read by candlelight anything smaller than the Ace of Spades'.

Back to School

————◆————

Imanaged to inveigle a girl-friend of mine into taking shooting lessons with me. She didn't want her husband to know about it (very sensibly: men get so barnacled into their territorial rights and suddenly feel all threatened if they think they're being invaded, and then there's that awful patronising guff: 'Ahhh, the little woman learning to shoot, quite sweet actually...') So rather than lie outright about where she was going each week, she told him she was taking up pottery to 'muck around with clays' which I thought was inspired.

Two seasons later – she must have found a decent pot-supplier as the husband apparently never twigged – and with the connivance of friends they were both, separately, asked to a day's shoot. Her husband watched, gratifyingly open-mouthed, as she was offered a peg number, pulled the borrowed school gun out from under a rug in the back of the car, and shot very commendably all day.

What they very wisely don't tell you at a shooting school when you start is that shooting has a learning-curve which, if you saw it as a graph, would deter you for ever. You learn the first steps, then you get stuck for what seems like an eternity; then a little more, then you get stuck again. Then, just when you think you've cracked it, you lose it all and it's back to the beginning again... It's a deeply depressing, slow, painful form of masochism.

Another deeply depressing aspect of starting to shoot clays is that you are then bulldozed into taking part in what are called charity shoots. You politely decline, but it's worse than trying to get out of making up a bridge four. 'Oh but you MUST, we desperately need one more and I KNOW you shoot... heavens no that doesn't matter a BIT none of us is any good either, and it IS for charity after all and it'll be VEY VEY relaxed and lots of chums...' And lo and behold, the day cometh and there are 30 teams of four and proper scoring cards and huge boards with everyone's names where your scores are written up for public scrutiny and comment, and it's frightfully jolly and amusing with lots of joshing and cries of 'AHA, the ladies' team, now that'll put us all to shame huhuhuh' and you wish to God that you were sitting quietly thinking your own thoughts in, for instance, Timbuktu instead of having agreed to take part in this crucifying agony*fest* and your nerves are rattling like castanets and all you want is to be able to throw a wobbly, quite noisily and publicly, and be taken away by nice men in white suits; and (moreover) realising that if 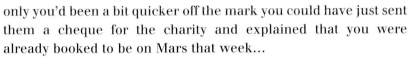 only you'd been a bit quicker off the mark you could have just sent them a cheque for the charity and explained that you were already booked to be on Mars that week...

Most people are terrific on these days, great sports who don't worry if they do badly, who take it all as just a bit of fun. *Which is what it's meant to be.* So how come I'm there trying not to throw up, and praying to every saint in the book that I won't make a complete fool of myself in public? Lack of confidence, too much self-regard – that's how. Plus the ardent desire not to see my name at the bottom of the list. It's just like being ten all over again, when the grown-ups said 'Well, somebody has to come last you know...' I know, I KNOW, but please please please don't let it be me...

People blithely tell you that all competitive clay courses are just a knack, once you've cracked the sequences. (Not with *Hélice* or 'ZZs' it isn't; this clay version of live pigeon shooting is universally recognised as being the most diabolically difficult discipline of all – just go and watch at what is, I think, the only permanent layout for it in this country, the West Kent Shooting School near Tunbridge Wells, where the British Grand Prix *Hélice* Championships are shot annually.) But whether it's *Hélice* or any other clay discipline – Doubles, Olympic trench, Down The Line, Skeet etc., or even sporting clays – practice is, quite simply, everything. As with so many little things, *n'est-ce pas*, the more you do it, the better you get...

Gentlemen, who've been shooting things with feathers on since they were nine, are utterly dismissive of such practices, and of shooting schools in general. 'Huh. Waste of time and money.' Not so. Shooting schools are perfectly wonderful for practice, for tweaking up the swing, sorting out the footwork, reminding you of what you should be doing. Like collies or collar stiffeners, they tidy up the line and get everything properly into place again. 'AND nothing like the real thing, dammit...' Fair enough: by its very nature a clay disc – even one in the best sporting layout – can never exactly mimic the bird it represents. It is slowing down rather than accelerating; it is smaller, and therefore, perversely, easier to focus on, with a shiny surface, a fraction of which always catches the light and gives you something to look for (rather than the beak of a live bird which you may not get to see anyway); it has no wings, so you are never distracted by extraneous movement nor by any optical illusion of a bird's size/speed, nor by trying feverishly to distinguish cocks from hens.

And clays invariably, even when the traps are moved around, appear from an appointed place and at an appointed height. They also are monitored by an instructor who knows what he's doing and is trying his damnedest to help you, exclusively (which you can't always say of the Almighty, to be fair) and who can repeat precisely the same target for you as often as required, so that you learn how to correct on it. And you are usually there only for a timed session, which means you're concentrating like mad and just going for broke, firing more or less continuously and with all the adrenalin fizzing, so if you miss a few it's not critical.

The other thing a shooting school doesn't simulate is the frequent weariness, the tedium of the Real Thing; the long, long waits; the fact that nothing happens for perhaps fifteen minutes after the drive has begun; the drives on which perhaps you never even lift your gun to a bird; when you are cold or wet or frozen to the marrow or possibly even just bored, when your mind starts to wander and you are beginning to think of other things – anything really – the landscape, shopping lists, what videos to take out tomorrow, how a hot bath would be just the ticket right now... And then, finally, a bird gets up, miles away, a high single cock bird, and it's making for you and the whole line is watching... I had just that, the last day out: waiting for the optimum angle, then up with the gun and cheek on the stock, and bang, a perfect textbook shot.

Only thing was, I'd failed to push off the safety catch. You cannot replicate the humiliation of that in a shooting school.

Pigeons Behaving Badly

I had a lovely couple of days' pigeon shooting earlier this year in June, when the showers and the winds as well as some good weather made the birds fly well and in profusion, albeit not necessarily over my hide. Just as well really, I'm hopeless at this. I kept wishing that Professor Garfit were with me to hand out helpful advice, as my *compadres* in the hide weren't much use: there was lots of 'Ahhh, old Archie Coats would have loved that one' which didn't help at all; and people saying things like 'You know, pigeons are the BEST practice for every different type of shooting – hit them and you can hit anything.' And as I can't, I obviously can't, if you see what I mean.

At least the daughter, who'd kindly volunteered to be in charge of the commissariat, had ensured we had the perfect picnic – flasks of tea and coffee, bottled water and lots of Crunchies, a box of beautifully-burned honey-covered sausages (not forgetting the Dijon) and two varieties of baps, ham or smoked salmon. It's not that I think about food *all* the time, you understand, but that was just the thing to keep body and soul together as you sat there waiting in the intermittent down-pours with Niagras sluic-

ing off the hat-brim, despondently working out what you should be doing, and wishing you were doing it tucked up in an armchair by a fire somewhere else... She had also very thoughtfully lent me a miniature radio with a single ear-piece but frankly I didn't feel it was Quite The Thing to be seen using, regardless of the programme.

Added to which of course, pigeon are totally *noiseless* birds. You're gazing over miles and miles of beautiful undulating countryside, with only the odd pylon to mess up the view, and screwing up your eyes to pick out flittering wings over distant hedges when suddenly, half a dozen birds – who've come in silently to the decoys below the sightline of the hide – are now gorging happily right bang in front of you... It makes one feel rather foolish.

Living for a time in Spain many moons ago, I'd once been taken to see a live-pigeon shoot near Madrid. It's a competitive event, held in a circular arena, wherein a series of birds is thrown out of a sort of box or pit in front of the firer, who then has to down each bird before it reaches (or falls into) the safety of the outer of the two circles drawn around the arena, when it is then deemed to have escaped. The 'art' of the thrower in the pit was to chuck the bird out in a manner which made a shot at it as difficult as possible (although now the birds are ejected automatically and at the push of a button) and this used to be effected by pulling out some wing feathers, or indeed breaking a wing, before the bird was thrown, which obviously caused it to fly unevenly and erratically.

Live pigeon shooting used to take place in Britain (there are wonderful photographs taken in 1894 of the International Meeting held in Notting Hill, as well as of others in Hornsby and Battersea and the Hurlingham Green Club) although it was later banned on grounds of cruelty by the Captive Birds Act of 1922, when clays and the *Hélice* discipline replaced the live birds. However live pigeon shooting still flourishes in certain European countries and places like Marrakesh. It is an extremely difficult 'target' sport as well as being a hugely social event entailing serious prize money, a lot of betting and much champagne in the spectator stands.

A little while after my first encounter with live pigeon shooting in Spain, I was living with friends in a lovely old *finca* near Seville. A pigeon struggled in to the belfry one Monday morning.

Whatever the farmers may think of them, pigeons as individuals are rather charming birds. This one had obviously escaped perdition from the activities of the local live-pigeon enthusiasts, who, as was the general custom, practised their sport every weekend in the nearby village. We tended the bird, put its wing in a splint, and offered it the sole tenancy of a large padded sewing basket in which it sat recuperating and being fed by means of a dropper. It was thoroughly amenable, joining in the conversation generally and, after a week or so, refreshed and looking for a bit of action, it joined in family life with gusto.

Morning shavers would be joined in the bathroom by Paco, karooing affectionately on a shoulder and interfering with the shaving foam. He would have lunch with us in the shade of the terrace, and his afternoon siesta would be taken perched on the end of one of the large old brass beds and going to sleep like everyone else. An early-evening session by the pool was greatly enjoyed, fending off the rude and jealous attentions of the dogs with the occasional well-aimed nip whilst making the most of the *tapas* of cheese or baked snails or freshly-toasted almonds. But most of all Paco enjoyed the bull-fighting programmes on the television, when he would strut excitedly up and down the back of a sofa, vocalising loudly to the rousing music of the *paso-dobles*, '*Marciál, eras lo mas grande*' being a particular favourite.

Occasionally he would fly out in the patio where he'd made friends with the roller-doves, or go for an evening flight with some chums. This effectively put a stop to any of our shooting forays in the fields of course, as it was too disconcerting, having to yell '*Paco*' at each lot of pigeons as they came in to the crops, just in case. If indeed he was with that particular group however, he'd swerve off immediately and come and join you in the hide, karooing delightedly at having come across you in so fortuitous a manner and, having tenderly nibbled your ear and re-arranged the feathers in your hat, would then drop down to the floor of the hide and play put-and-take with the empty cartridge cases. He clearly preferred being with the grown-ups to being with any of his own kind. A very civilised bird. Then, one morning, an odd thing happened.

It was at breakfast when, as usual, he was busy under the table pecking for crumbs and investigating toes. Suddenly there was a lot of flurrying and hiccupping going on, I looked under the table, and there was Paco, looking somewhat shifty, with an egg under him. Still warm, and indisputably newly-laid. To give him credit, he never looked at it afterwards, and seemed very anxious to disown the whole embarrassing episode, in the manner of one who has temporarily, and rather unfortunately, let wind pass, or suffered a slight hormonal crise, but is anxious to reassure his friends that it won't occur a second time.

These things happen in the best-regulated circles. None of us ever referred to it again in his presence.

Driven to Distraction

My father, tall, blue-eyed and extremely good-looking, could never have been mistaken for anything other than an officer and an Englishman. His best suits (which he only wore in the evening – 'no point in wearing out expensive cloth on London pavements I always say, off the peg's good enough for meetings with the riffraff') were built for him by Johns & Pegg, his best shoes were by Lobb. The only tunes he ever hummed, in a firm and totally unmelodious manner, were Gilbert & Sullivan's. He would stand to attention for the national anthem on television, and wept unashamedly on Remembrance Sunday and at Trooping the Colour. He had gone to India after Sandhurst, was in Palestine as an ADC, took the Poles into Tobruk and later was with Glubb in the desert. He maintained that he had had 'an amusing' war and then joined the diplomatic service as a Q.M. in order that he might continue to travel. We were stationed in Egypt for several years. His greatest loves were the three generations of females in his family, boats, cricket and shooting, reading aloud, which he did beautifully, anything even remotely funny and banana mess.

He was also probably the world's worst driver. After the war, all of which he had spent in the Middle East, he had a series of vintage motorcars. He drove any vehicle much as he would, I imagine, have driven a car through the desert – casually, almost unthinkingly, untroubled of regulations and for fun – in a rather grand if cavalier fashion somewhat reminiscent of characters in a Dornford Yates novel ('Berry gently lifted his foot off the clutch and the great car leapt forward'.) A humorous, gentle and kind character, he only very occasionally ever raised his voice in anger, when he was patently at the end of his tether. Behind the wheel therefore he was generally placid but basically disliked, and therefore dismissed, other road-users. He drove for the sheer pleasure of driving, and other vehicles were just a nuisance, blots on the perfect landscape.

One of his last and most beloved cars was a very ancient and beautiful Bentley with a walnut fascia and flip-up indicators, immaculately kept, which he used to go down and say goodnight to every evening and which he drove, as always, with fine insouciance. Bicyclists down country lanes fell off their machines into ditches as he roared past majestically, politely acknowledging their consideration with a regal wave. He had the most beautiful manners, only very occasionally misdirected and, a stranger to road-rage, it was a rare occasion when he ever came near to losing his cool about another driver, at which point you knew it was serious. 'O *get* out of the way' he would mutter, foot hard down to overtake an articulated truck on a hill-bend before swerving violently in front of its screeching brakes in the teeth of on-coming traffic who all flashed their lights and stood on their horns. 'No courtesy, that fellow, really, he should have pulled over to let me through. Extremely dangerous.' 'But pa...' I would start to say, faintly – 'Darling, please don't talk while I'm in the middle of a tricky manoeuvre, it's rather distracting'.

Somewhat understandably, in view of his love of the open road, he disliked having to drive in town, and for any passenger the journey became even more of a nightmare. Accelerating

gracefully away from the lights, ('ahh, good, our turn now' he'd purr in a pleased tone) he looked neither to right or left and tardy pedestrians were blithely ignored. Terrorised old ladies with shopping baskets would be seen leaping like gazelles out of his path and unwary motorcyclists found themselves careering into bollards or mounting pavements. 'Watch out pa, there's a... oh never mind ...' ; a goods-van, breaking hard to avoid him, swerved into a line of parked cars and the air rang with the sound of crunching glass and metal, shouts, horn-blowing and invectives. 'What was that darling? Sorry, concentrating on something else... yes, you have to watch out like a hawk you know, half these people have no idea *at all* of what they're doing. Absolute menace.'

He would have been mortified however if you'd even hinted that his driving wasn't up to snuff. As we were making the usual splendid, if erratic, progress through a large town early one Saturday morning, actually on our way to a shoot together, a lorry with French number plates got cut up on my father's side. The enraged driver blasted the horn and, leaning out of his window, started screaming and gesticulating, violently and (I thought) fairly graphically. We had guns and cartridges in the back and I had visions of An Incident... Pa was totally unfazed. 'I wonder what he wants – directions, I imagine... really? ... oh, um... how unpleasant – well, never mind. Anyway, he was in the way and we can't be late can we – not for a shooting day.' No gentleman, he maintained, was ever late for the monarch, the church or a shooting engagement.

He was as deaf as a stone (which presumably accounted for much of his blithe indifference in traffic, come to think of it) thanks to the war and, probably, too many days out with a shotgun after. 'Whatever do I want with one of those wretched things?' he would counter, when his family regularly tried to beg or bully him into getting a hearing aid, for their sakes as much as his. 'Certainly not. I can hear everything I need to hear.' And he could too, which was so maddening – like dogs who are deaf to all admonishments but who can hear the opening of the food bin from 300 yards. He was oblivious to a telephone, or an alarm-clock, or a plea to help moving furniture, or anything he didn't really like, yet out shooting he could hear the grass grow. Typical Englishman, really.

Game for the Fair

Game Fair fever strikes again. Decisions, decisions... What to take: spade and bottled water in boot, of course. Smelling salts, umbrella. Oh, and balloon for attaching to roof-aerial as Idiot's Aid, so as to avoid perennial evening panic in car park. What to wear...? Will it be jungle weather as per couple of years ago? (Probably hormonal, but I almost died of heatstroke; how come P. of Wales managed to saunter out of whirly-bird, looking irritatingly cool and indahouse in double-breasted grey check and making genial chat to ferrets, while everyone else's scarlet faces dripped like taps?) Or will it be a re-run of Famous Floors '88 when scuba equipment was needed, every trade-stand looked like it'd been used for mud wrestling, and a great wind got up on the last evening, hurling both the tea tent into a tree and an extremely bemused cow onto the local railway line?

Dawn sortie obviously *de rigeur* to try and avoid usual nose-to-tail frenzy on local roads. In the days of King John, a squirrel could travel from the Severn to the Humber without touching ground, and probably in less time than it'll take me even to reach Hammersmith flyover... I bet squirrels never had tree-rage. Fair traffic now is always ghastly. Especially those demonic, aggressive queue-barging drivers, pushing and swearing and revving and in a lather, displaying every trait of pre-cosmic biology – which was based on the premise that 'mere existence is no proof of intelligent life-form' – and each with an IQ so small it really shouldn't be allowed out on its own...

Once inside the Fair however, everything is more or less sweetness and light. Of course there's always going to be someone who complains about something, like the rubbish not being collected often enough, or the state of the ground which means the glassware-stand is on an incline and all the stock keeps slithering off the shelves; or the intersection taps that have run out of water. Or the time all the hay-bales, which hadn't been properly netted up, started to disintegrate and blow about, to the incandescent fury of that year's stately-home owner. Or the first year, remember?, that the French had a little enclave of their own, with those gorgeous hunting horns sounding their tremulous *rallyes*, (the *chasse par force* and the *chasse du cerf* or *du sanglier*), and stalls selling cheeses and champagne and wonderful leather goods and antique French prints – all of which was admirable except that none of them took cheques or credit cards and there was such a run on cash in the mobile banks it might have been 1929 all over again with people throwing themselves out of caravan windows...

But, generally, everyone's happy. Highland cattle, deer, goats and woolly sheep the size of Morris Minors gaze out of pens, the knobs and the knockers rub shoulders in the wine bars and eat smoked salmon sandwiches or trout-mousse baps whilst the tattooed brigade go for hamburgers and beer. Cheering crowds watch the displays in the main arena; purveyors of country clothing, 4x4 vehicles, stuffed owls, antique books, rearing equipment, thumb-sticks, garden furniture and dog-beds are all doing a brisk

trade – the retail index must be going through the roof. Attendants at the trade stands and marquees taken by estate agents, art galleries, countryside associations, gunmakers, sporting magazines, hedge-layers and auction-houses are pouring drinks down their, or somebody else's, clients; and people who only see each other here, once a year, meet and greet old friends. The food and craft tents, the fishing tackle emporia and the casting demonstrations down on the water are all crammed with punters; and flags fly everywhere.

There are the usual weary announcements over the loudspeaker for owners to collect dogs or children and remove their illegally-parked cars from behind the stands; the regulars have managed to borrow badges again and sneak past the uniformed sergeant into the CLA loos which are of course, with the band playing in the enclosure just outside, the choicest around. But no-one gets overly aerated about such minor misdemeanours. People say 'good-morning' to each other and gentlemen raise their hats, there are pretty girls in prints and battle-axes in wrap-around Barbour skirts and ancient colonels in moustaches and keepers in tweeds and clay-pigeon enthusiasts toting shotgun-slips; strawhatted officials with regimental buttons on their blazers meet for breakfast in the marquees, and Innes plays his pipes every morning at nine. And if you strung all the dog-leads being used, end to end, they would altogether measure more than the length of the country.

Every year, whatever the venue, whatever the weather, you return from trudging round the Fair wearier, hoarser, vastly poorer and what feels like three feet shorter, but triumphant. Once again, it's been worth it. Unlike the Puskar fair in Rajasthan, which regularly gets broken up by rioting camels; or San Fermin, where the number of deaths – although publicly frowned on by the Spanish authorities – merely serves as an indicator of the quality of the year's *criada* of bulls; or the Rural in Argentina, where blood-feuds are always settled in the llama tents and the gauchos' *criollo* ponies invariably stampede through the hot-dog stalls and the tango dancers, the Game Fair is not the venue for thrills, spills, rowdiness or wild excess. Or cats. It is, after all, the quintessential British country fair.

Big Bandobast

U p to Scotland for the summer bucket-and-spade holidays with children and lovely uncomplicated friends who just want to laze around, take a barbecue off to the beach, read, paint and do nothing in particular. It's also the best time, for me, for the annual much-needed purge – getting the place sorted-out before the stalking and shooting seasons begin, chucking out and re-sorting and tidying corners and outbuildings that have been used by everyone as a general dump for the past twelve months; the sort of exercise that was known in India in my father's day as 'Making Big Bandobast'.

The chimneys will have already been done in the spring, thank heavens. The old way of cleaning a chimney was for some-one to sit on the roof and let down 'a bit rope' on which would be tied a big bunch of heather, and then yank the whole lot up. The only things that have cleared our chimneys for years are the birds who snuggle in for warmth at the top, get woozy from the smoke and then fall straight down. One day I found Annie (who 'does') covered in filth and screeching blue murder, having chased a small, equally filthy and very cross small owl round and round the sitting-room with a fishing net and, having cornered it, being then too frightened to pick it up. Wild birds do have a way of making their feelings perfectly obvious. Out shooting one winter, one of the girls had to disappear urgently behind a bush. Everyone tact-fully looked the other way. Suddenly there was a loud shriek fol-lowed by wild commotions in the undergrowth. She had appar-ently pulled everything down, crouched low and discovered she was sitting on a pheasant, who (somewhat natural-ly) retaliated.

Today, a tour round the yard and the out-buildings, and what in Scotland are called 'the policies'. Clearly the now-defunct electricity room's in urgent need of refurbishment. Can't have been touched in years. Hoses, a derelict doll's house, archaic horse tackle, children's

bicycles, boxes of chains, even a ruined bath inhabited by dead leaves and a glum-looking toad, huddle under heaps of empty feeding-bags and decayed pheasant netting. There's a gas-mask lurking in a chamber-pot and a rowing boat propped up in one corner. The old deer-saddles and the panniers are at least hung up above mouse-level but there's an astonishing collection of spavined tables and decrepit kitchen chairs, very gone in the back legs, as well as lots of weevily wartime moss baskets, jars and jars of rusty nails, dead papers and piles of broken glass. Not a pretty sight. All that's needed is a nice day, loads of energy and some rubber gloves, but it makes you feel weak just contemplating such an Augean task – demolishing a time-warp.

The other horror is an anachronism called the Plucking

Room, where game-birds were dealt with in my father-in-law's time. One of the older ladies of the household, now long since dead, confessed, during an evening of much liquid refreshment when we were celebrating her 86th birthday, to having been ravished in there by the boot-boy – '1917 it was, I mind it well'. It is now a creepy little room, all romance fled – full of scythes and peat-spades and rolls of wire and ferret-boxes; there are small animal skins pinned out on boards, tins of evil-smelling black viscous stuff, bits of chough hanging off a nail next to rusty saws and blades, buckets full of smashed clam shells and sorcerers' implements in huge galvanised iron pots. There is also a fine collection of those old green ribbed glass bottles with printed labels marked 'POISON, only to be used for...' to which some wit once added the words 'The Factor' in scrawly ink. No-one would dare clean out those horrors – the room really needs dynamiting.

Back in the house, where the usual amount of mess has accumulated over the year. Shan't touch the wine-cellar, though – last time was a disaster. A few months after getting married it was, and in a timely fit of new-wifely enthusiasm I thought I'd be really helpful and attack the spiders there, in the process of which I broke a bottle of what turned out to be horribly ancient brandy.

Annie and I were mopping madly, and getting hysterically merry on the fumes, when in walks the laird after a day out on the hill, takes in the scene – the spillage, the smell, the shards of glass everywhere, the broken wax stopper – and is silent. I start to babble guiltily – the bottle had been on the floor behind the door, just awful, never even saw it till it broke, entirely my fault and I'm so very sorry – crikey, was that really what it was – God how *dreadful* and I'm terribly *terribly* sorry but I thought I was being so helpful... just *can't* apologise enough... Serious, abject grovel.

He was going pucer by the minute, and was now staring at me as if at a ghost. Something then snapped. 'I don't care HOW you did it, I want to know WHY you did it' he yelled. By this time I felt I'd made my point and had done quite enough of the back-lashing; and, being still somewhat carefree thanks to the fumes, it seemed the right moment to bring this little episode to an end. 'Oh, I don't know' I replied, a mite too airily perhaps, 'I just saw the bottle lying there and *jumped* on it.' Huge mistake. 'You DIDN'T' he gasped. I thought he was going to have a seizure.

Since then I've cleaned the basement and the attics, and the yards and the log-stores and the stables and the gutters, and I've learned how to gralloch a beast and clean a fish but I've never, ever, touched the cellar again.

But the gun-room definitely needs a going-over. That I can do: whisk the dead spiders out of the backs of drawers, hoover the remains of moths off the baize in the glass-fronted erstwhile gun cabinets in which (now that we all have to have proper security cabinets for firearms) general paraphernalia is now stored; the shelves of books and pamphlets, game-books and record-sheets, invoices and larder receipts from knife-manufacturers and game merchants, all need sorting, plus the year's collection of magazines and cryptic messages which are now history. There are strange phials in plastic boxes marked *Institute samples: close firmly*; boxes of roe jaws and some owl pellets, packets of tags for

carcasses and an impressive hoard of used brown paper; brass cartridges waiting to be re-loaded; paper targets, a roll of maps, and some eagles' feathers, stuck up in the cobwebs decorating a set of antlers over the door ... And there are all the ancient brass-cornered cartridge magazines, and the cartridge bags and the telescopes in their leather cases, and the grandfather's leg-o'-mutton gun cases, and the big old double gun cases, which can now be steeped in leather oil and polished until they gleam. That's my favourite job, and listening to Donald's stories as we work.

We beaver away, sorting and clearing, fortified by mugs of tea.

It's a long job, mainly because every bit of paper, every dog-eared photograph unearthed, gets minutely examined and stories emerge like goblins from each. 'Hey Prof, isn't that the Major with the fish he poached from below the bridge, the day you and I got the Land Rover stuck in the river?' 'Aye, by God it is, and the next day we got that big old goat up by the lighthouse, mind? And we only had a tin of pineapple juice between us an' it was a scorcher, and Miss Sylvia'd gone and lost the flask…'

There are the inevitable collection of prints, pictures and maps on the walls, together with safety notices, charts of weights and bullet-drop diagrams, lists of suppliers and carriers and feed-merchants and purveyors of almost everything, as well as cuttings and silly poems and cartoons. And photographs pinned up behind the door: a barbecue by the loch when the ferrets escaped; the daughter's first rabbit held aloft in triumph; groups standing by the big iron target up the glen; the dog singing under the Christmas tree; an immortal Macnab consisting of a wild goat, a saithe and a Peruvian hat with a feather pinned into it… endless memorabilia, each with its own story demanding to be re-told.

In the back of one of the shelves above the work bench, behind the First Aid kit, the flares and the anti-midge stuff, sits a bottle of whisky. There is always a bottle of whisky there – for the regulation dram, or because it's dawn and you need a nip before going out on a marauder hunt, or in case of sudden faintness, or a celebration – who cares? It does wonders for the remaining cold tea so we help ourselves liberally. Must be gone six by now, I sent the obedient house-party off for a day at the beach on the other side of the island, and Donald and I have been at this since morning.

'Shall we do those boxes under there, or call it a day?' 'Och fer God's sake wifey, away wid ye and have yer bath, yer folks'll be back any time now…ye're covered in dust and spider-webs an' ye look like hell. We'll finish this tomorrow, mebbe…' Maybe.

Marking Time

very year in Scotland, in earliest summer and amongst the lovely hills and folds of the big glen, a group of match rifle friends and enthusiasts gather together to spend a week shooting at a target, at distances of between 1,500 yards and one and a half miles.

It's not quite as daft as it sounds. Each distance is marked out along the winding glen track by a raised, square, turfed firing point, and there are several wind-flags set up on appropriate contours of the hills. The target itself, 20ft wide by 10ft high and standing on the rising ground which itself is covered in quarry dust, is constructed of mild steel and with the normal 'match-rifle' scoring rings painted on it, all except for the 'V-bull' – the ortho-centre of the bull's-eye ring – which is an old gong bolted out from the surface of the target and which, when hit, clangs most rewardingly. There is a concrete-lined marker's gallery dug out some twenty feet below, and 20 feet or so away from, the face of the target, in which the markers – usually a couple of the more longsuffering members of the party – sit, fortified by sandwiches and a flask, communicating via radio back to the firing party and calling out the value of each shot fired. At the end of a string of say 20 shots, firing ceases; the All Clear is given and confirmed, and the markers emerge like moles from the gallery to patch the bul-let-holes with the aid of some putty, a ladder, a large brush and a tin of whitewash. This done, they scurry back into the butt, radio back to the others, and the next firer begins.

It's a leisurely, easy way to spend the days. The party is lazy, relaxed and good-humoured, there's no sense of urgency or rush. Each firing point can only accommodate two people at most; one shooting, the other coaching, keeping the score, watching the shot through the spotting 'scope, seeing the dust puff up if the bul-let strikes low, calling the wind, calculating elevations, arguing fiercely about who's got it wrong. The other members of the party lie about in the heather, sleeping off the previous evening's dis-cussion with the port or the malt, sketching, reading, declaiming verse, doing the crossword whilst keeping an eye on the picnic baskets and the beer and wine cooling in a nearby stream; or just chuntering away happily about – oh, anything at all; from how Galileo was correct ('as indeed we have proved by experimenta-tion in this very glen') when he wrote in 1637 that 'the shot goes furthest when the elevation is 45% or, as they say, in the sixth quadrant', to whether it's worth taking a rod out later on and if so who's going to row... Or indeed just shouting unhelpful com-ments to those hard at work on the firing point, or gossiping over the radio with the markers, and making unflattering comments about the wind-coaching so far...

Sometimes this desultory chat is actually quite useful: when shooting from the mile-and-a-half firing point, you need all the help you can get. The shot takes eight seconds to reach the target – you look in to the scope on '7' and if it's a hit the paint falls off, it's very satisfying – so at the moment of the shot, someone tells the marker: 'right; on aim… shot's gone' and everyone holds their breath. And if, after 8 seconds, there's a yell and 'aha ya bugger, it's a bloody ringing bull' comes back over the air, then pandemonium ensues and everything stops for the regulation dram. Although this is an M.O.D.-approved 'range', it's a far cry from Stickledown and the pressure – and discipline – of serious competitions.

On normal firing ranges, communications between the firing point and the marker-butts are formal, short, precise and simple. All communications, or instructions, are called 'Messages', and each Message has, for clarity's sake, its own designated number. As there can be anything up to 50 targets being used at the same time in any one detail, the Message number will be prefixed by the number of the Target to which it refers. So 'All targets: Message 1' means 'All targets: Up' at the beginning of a detail; equally: 'Target 36, Message 10' means that, on Target 36, shooting has finished and its marker can stand down. But the message that most frequently emanates from the firing point (especially when the wind is changing fast and it all gets tricky) is 'Message 4'. This means you've let off your shot, but the marker on your target hasn't seen it or signalled its score; so 'Target 8, Message 4' is the acknowledged way for the firer on Target 8 to alert that particular marker on the lines of 'Wake up, sunshine, I've fired a perfectly good shot, probably a bullseye; now *look* at the target and *find* the hole. Please'. You then wait and pray that the thing has actually connected somewhere – anywhere would do – as of course the reply 'Clear target' would mean *nul points.*

In days of yore during Match Rifle competitions in the Bisley Imperial Meeting, competitors would sometimes also have to do marking duties when the usual paid markers were unavailable. A detail would be divided in two, the top half would mark for the bottom half and then vice versa. Amongst those doing marking duty below the parapet one particular morning were some very senior members of the shooting world. Back at the firing point, somebody was clearly making a horlicks on Target 24 – lots of anxious 'Target 24, Message 4' pleas were winging down to the butts, to each of which came the reply 'Clear Target'. Finally, in desperation, the firer demanded 'Target 24, Message 5'; and

'Message 5' means 'I challenge for a hit'. This meant that Target 24 had to be lowered yet again, but this time the Butt Officer, together with anyone else who might be termed a figure of authority, had to examine it and try and find a shot-hole.

The following day, the incident was reported in *The Times* in these words:

'The shooter had again been signalled a miss and, clearly suspecting some slack marking, requested the target be re-examined. On being signalled a Clear Target, he challenged for a hit. After a long pause, whilst the target was pulled down for re-examination, the reply from the butts came back: "Convey to the firer on Target 24 that his target has been examined by the Butt Officer, and by a Canon of the Church, a Peer of the Realm, the Vice Chairman of Council and the Captain of the English Eight. And it is still clear."

Road-Worthy

The minute my daughter turned 21 she announced that she was going to get herself a vehicle to keep up at home on the island in Scotland. It seemed perfectly reasonable: she could then ferry round her own friends and wouldn't need to use the house car or borrow anyone else's transport. She knew exactly what she wanted and, no thank you, she would find it herself. It took about six months, but that autumn she was proudly lurching around in a seriously wrecked old Land Rover which looked as if it could well have figured on the *Mary Rose* cargo list, but which had been, she swore, thoroughly vetted – although I reckoned someone must have been bribed stupid to have given it any sort of certificate.

The thing hiccupped and spluttered and walloped its way round the place. It ground to a halt going through puddles (the brake pads didn't like water of any sort, and always seized up even after the shortest cloud-burst); it died going up hills; it guzzled fuel as if it was going out of fashion and always had smoke belching from one orifice or another. It wouldn't start if the weather was hot, and didn't work anyway if it was cold. In short, it was a total mechanical disaster but it was hers and, as they say in Scotland, 'she was in her glory'. I insisted she took a mobile phone whenever she was going out in it, made promises of a staggeringly large fiscal nature to St. Christopher, and hung out of the windows like Sister Ann, waiting for that sound of crashing oil drums and rattling old tin cans – you could hear it for miles, it was quite unmistakable – which meant, thank God, she was on her way back home again.

One year the boys down at the airport, at the southern end of the island, clubbed together and bought themselves a second hand single-engine two-seater plane. It was brought over rather ignominiously on the ferry on the back of a lorry – clearly the previous owner wanted nothing further to do with it – and once it had been delivered to the airfield we all drove down to have a look. It was ochre-yellow and white with an underbelly of a particularly malevolent shade of brown and it looked like a fried egg in a cowpat. It sat in the pleasant summer sun, shaking as if it had ague. Its canvas wings were ripped and shredded and held together by duck-tape; inside, both seats had been completely eaten by mice and of the three dials on the dashboard, none were readable as the glass on each was smashed and the dials were hanging out.

'Looks – well, *different*' I said; 'where did you get it?' 'Och it cum out tha' wee magazeeen – ye ken the wan – *Exchange an' Mart* it wuz. Sum find, eh?' 'Oh?' 'Aye, an' a reel bargain tu.' No kidding. My husband, who had logged up thousands of hours driving sensible aircraft round the skies, started to jog from foot to foot and looked shiftily at me. 'Erm... why don't you – um – just take the car home now' he said. 'One of the boys will give me a lift back – think I'll just stay on here for a bit, ok?' I made him swear on everything I could think of that he wouldn't fly it. Especially over the sea as the next stop's America and if he... oh well ... 'Hmm? oh *do* stop fussing, it'll be fine...'

A couple of hours later there was an extraordinary noise which seemed to be approaching the house from the seaward side. I cursed and rushed out to have a look. Duck-tape flapping gaily, the fried egg was airborne, flailing round in the air like some demented bronco. Bang, it went. *Chuckchuckchuckchuck... bang... Ffizzzzzz, pudderpudderpudder, whoop... pudderpudder... Ktchar, ktchar, ktchar... Ffftttt... pop.* He tried unsteadily to dip a wing as he passed and a gull screeched in alarm and dived for the sea. The egg lurched perilously over the roof and, still popping, disappeared again in a southerly direction... Suddenly everything was very quiet. 'Interesting, that,' he explained later 'no proper rudder control at all, you know; but great FUN.'

Just as there is something inherently endearing about old machines, conversely new ones are often regarded with deep suspicion. A visitor once turned up on the island in a spanking bright new silver Aston (which did look a bit out of place) and was promptly treated like a pariah by everyone: I felt rather sorry for him, but in fact he turned out to be total prat, even refusing to go and search for some girl's lost ring in the undergrowth as, he said, his 'chinos wouldn't like it'. So, on the morning he was due to leave on the ferry and whilst he was still in the bath, we tied some salmon skins to his manifold. It was a gorgeous hot day and we reckoned the thing would really start to hum once he'd driven off the ferry at the other end and was making the couple of hours' journey to his next port of call, a smart castle further up the west coast.

Once, staying with friends for a shoot in Hampshire, we all laid bets as to who would be the best shot of the day, based purely on their cars as they arrived. The winner by a mile arrived driving a filthy mini pick-up van, with a pair of his father's Boss's – with which he shot quite beautifully – hidden under an evil-smelling spaniel in the back. The worst shot of all was the owner of a new, all-dancing Range Rover with a London dealer's sticker in the back window, drawers for bottles and glasses built into the boot and personalised number-plates. He also had gold lettering on his gun slips. During the first ten minutes of the first drive, a total of twelve birds, completely ignoring the rest of the line, did a fly-past straight over him, one by one and at decent intervals apart. He missed them all. As the thirteenth approached, he was heard to groan 'O Christ, not another one.' The rest, as they say, is history.

We did once have a Hungarian to stay one winter in Scotland, who arrived rather nervously in a chauffeur-driven car off the ferry. He had, apparently, been hideously sick during the crossing, a fact attributed partly to the very rough seas and partly to the Macbrayne's fry-up of which he had unthinkingly partaken. Perhaps it was the memory of this, or indeed the sight of a good shooting breakfast the following morning in the house (porridge, black pudding, kedgeree and the like) but the Hungarian, a proud man, shot like a drain all day. He was invited, after the last drive, to shoot at a bonfire near the yard, which he also missed. 'In my cowntree' he announced gloomily, 'I vooda haf to shood myselva now, for de disgraice.' 'Aye, an ye'd miss that too nae doot' came the cheerful riposte from one of the gaggle of beaters, by now swigging drams by the back door.

The proud Hungarian left next morning in his chauffeur-driven car and was never heard of again.

Déjeuner sur l'Herbe

It was one of those summer evenings which somehow just rolls on and on – everybody in high spirits after a good day and a good dinner, raiding the grog tray and the old dressing-up box, playing sardines and high cockalorum, dancing the *salsa* and doing all the stupid things that all the best Scottish house-parties do, far into the night. Clearly no-one was going to bed, what with the *craic* and the drink and the music and the general bonhommie. Then about 5am someone complained of sudden hunger and Spasm – he's always known as Spasm – who, even when drunk and patently out of his skull, is both an opera buff with a passion for Wagner which verges on the idolatrous *and* an extraodinarily able cook – offered to produce breakfast so long as we ate it out on the lawn and watched the dawn break *and* his favourite composer was on the machine at full volume through the open windows to accompany this *fête gastronomique*. We all proceeded solemnly out onto the dew-sodden grass to tortured waves of *Lohengrin*, clutching chairs, a table, Buck's fizz and plates piled high with scrambled anchovied eggs and toast, to be instantly set

upon by whining hordes of midges enjoying an early breakfast of their own. I fled
after three minutes but the others loyally
sat it out, munching toast with added
midges in a sort of group-therapy way
and making complimentary noises
about both the chef and the dawn.

Eating out of doors, even when fending off the local fauna,
does have something special about it. Probably the first hunting
picnic recorded was in the 15th century when Gaston de Foix, in
Le Livre de Chasse, wrote of tables being set up by the hunt servants in the forest, at which the stag-hunters would feast on fresh-
ly-killed venison after the rigours of the chase. Not unlike those
Yee Haw Trigger-burger stalls at rodeos, come to think of it. I
maintain that the secret of good outdoor food is to make it uncomplicated – all that Edwardian paraphernalia involving parasols,
wickerwork, jelly moulds, cream cakes, tiny sandwiches, itsy-
bitsy dishes, candles, sweetmeats and cutlery is not good news.
Men anyway basically like simple fare when they're picnicking,
anything that can be eaten in the fingers: nothing complicated,
nothing that has to be held the right way up or involves teaspoons
and, above all, nothing which involves them in any sort of clear-
ing-up after. I had the best-ever picnic once in Yorkshire where
I'd been invited to join the fishing party. We all sat on the river
bank, accompanied by some sheep complaining insistently in the
local vernacular and, whilst several fat wild brown trout were
grilling slowly on a fire, we had gulls' eggs, fresh baguettes and
local cheese, and drank quantities of river-chilled beer and wine.
The afternoon faded into somewhat of a blur afterwards, but it
was perfection.

Stalking 'pieces' are different and everyone has their own
favourite. Here again though, the vital elements are simplicity
combined with a certain robustness – something capable of being
carried in a pocket, lain on without inflicting hospitalisation and
then submerged without noticeable effect if you have to stand
waist-deep in a burn; and which, if not being exactly a visual
delight, is at least recognisable when you are finally allowed to
stop and have it. So, no whole tomatoes for instance, and
absolutely nothing hard, leakable or fiddly; a couple of generously-

filled baps, plus some chocolate and a slice of fruitcake, is ideal.

We once hired a cook for the season who, despite careful instructions, obviously hadn't quite grasped the stalkers' needs. On her first morning, before I'd even had chance to check, she'd sent a stalking guest out with chicken satay, buttered oatcakes and cream cheese, together with a rather pretty avocado dip, all carefully and individually wrapped inside a plastic bag. Yep. Fate took a hand: the guest, having duly stowed his packed lunch in a back pocket, climbed into the stalker's car and instantly, with a howl of agony, found his right buttock impaled on a couple of wooden skewers which had torn through the plastic bag, having already penetrated the package containing the avocado dip. It's amazing how deep a wound can be inflicted, even through tweed and in the sturdiest buttock, by a satay stick in a confined area; the resulting mess of blood, chicken bits, sauce, avocado and cream-cheese-on-oatcakes, which hadn't survived impact either and now looked like regurgitated hen-litter, was indescribable.

Another day, again out stalking, I discovered that my piece consisted of half a pink, juicy, cold grouse. How lovely, I thought, nothing better. Donald and I shared it voraciously when, as so often happens, the mist came down and it came on to rain. We sheltered cosily behind a rock, mumbling happily between mouthfuls and picking on the bones like the Twa Corbies, when all of a sudden came the roar of a stag nearby. What luck! Hurriedly grabbing rifle and binoculars, we crawled to the brow of the hill to spy what was, indeed, a very shootable stag. 'Take him quickly now, he'll no' wait long.' But it wasn't that easy – I didn't seem to be able to hold the rifle, my fingers were slipping and slithering as I cursed and fumbled madly with the safety catch that wouldn't shift, and Donald swore as the binoculars skidded from his grasp... Then, suddenly, he started to chortle as we both simultaneously realised the obvious fact that you simply cannot hold onto anything, let alone squeeze a trigger, if your hands are smothered in *jus de volaille*.

'Wail,' he said philosophically as we cursed our stupidity, 'Ah seen grouse ruin a stalk afore now, but never a bloody *cooked* one. *Slainte*, anyroads,' and we drowned our sorrows in the traditional manner.

Pot Luck

———◆———

Talking about food, it is such a vital part of shooting and stalking that I wonder a book hasn't yet been written about it. Not game recipes, but a history of the meals themselves, the enormous feasts that must have been given after a Tainchel, or when Louis XV or Gaston de Phoebus or Elizabeth I went hunting. Edward Duke of York, the grandson of Edward III, who wrote that great English hunting treatise, *The Master of Game*, between 1406 and 1413 – one of the earliest and most important works on hunting in the English language, albeit much of it extracted from Gaston de Foix's earlier *Livre de Chasse* – makes no mention whatsoever of breaking his fast, either in the forest or afterwards. There would have been, in some cases, bowers, musicians (think of those sheets of hunting music, illustrated in such detail – the *Musique de Chasse, de Vénerie, de la Chasse par Force; tons lorsque les chiens emportent; tons pour la Queste; pour le Hallaly*) and afterwards, the *tableaux* of game; but yet, no music for the feast? Come to think of it, the only culinary details we have about those enormous early hunts are the facts that the beasts were roasted on spits for the gentry and that the peasants got the numbles to make into pies.

Stalking is, obviously, the poor relation when it comes to making merry over the victuals. It's not a sport for feasting at. One of the few people actually recorded as having eaten anything at all on the hill is Charles St. John of whom it was told that, having followed the Muckle Hart of Ben More for six days before killing it, he 'shot a couple of grouse with one shot from his rifle which he speedily skinned... and took to the burn to wash them' before cooking them on a small fire.

Latterly, from the 19th century onwards, shooting luncheons are better documented. Oyster banquets for Edward VII, and meals of five courses at Hall Barn in Buckinghamshire hosted by Lord Burnham; the invention of The King's Ginger due to Queen Victoria's disapproval of her son's liberal intake of noxious and inebriating whisky in the shooting field; the teas, and the tea-gowns, of a shooting party, followed by evening dress for a dinner sometimes consisting of 16 separate dishes. The keepers and beaters were traditionally given 'a rabbit apiece' (and doffed their caps, murmuring in unison 'we thank your Grace') which must have looked pretty measly on that famous day at Blenheim on October 7th 1898, when 6943 rabbits were shot.

Nowadays it is usually on the Continent that you find houses in which the *déjeuner de chasse* still rivals anything we might think more appropriate to the great Edwardian days of shooting hospitality. Eleven o'clock in the morning, and you are shown through to a dining room in full splendour with figurines placed down the centre of the table – hunting dogs, stags, roe deer, boar and game birds in silver or Meissen or bronze or, once, memorably, in gold. *Patés* of hare and duck, smoked meats (goose breast, venison, suckling pig) and hot bone-marrow on toast; saddle of wild boar and of roe; *croissants*, pastries, *compotes* and *tartines*, salads and cheeses, followed perhaps by some *tartes aux myrtilles*, fruits and figs, or crystallised ginger with fresh thick cream; and six sets of crystal for the finest champagne and wines. You then stagger out into the freezing cold and, rather disconcertingly, start shooting at half past two.

Even when it's a lunch *champètre*, it can either be held in a tent with waiters in white gloves as was customary in the old days of partridge-shooting in Spain when the Jockey Club from Madrid catered, and served, the smartest shoots; or it is perhaps a huge barbecue, tended by liveried staff plying your goblets with flagons of mulled wine... It's a tough life but someone has to do it.

Mind you that's abroad – we do things rather differently here, my dear: nothing OTT, nothing that might be termed 'trying a bit too hard', knowwhatImean? Goodness me yes. And I'm not whingeing or anything, and God knows we've all had our off-days in the kitchen, but it's the packet soup, and those hard little bread rolls like Jurassic droppings, and the bit of tired railway cake, that are the real bummers aren't they? And the beaters all sitting hunched and silent in the barn, rain dripping through the rafters, tearing up their own squashed sandwiches to share with the dogs. Happy sporting days, eh?

But it's as well to know. An Englishman, you have to remember, likes really simple things for his shooting lunch, and preferably in the company of other men. Hare pie (albeit a trifle fancy, perhaps?) or a decent casserole – even ham doorsteps with mustard, or a ploughman's lunch at the local, followed by a wedge of mousetrap and some beer and claret. Nothing foreign. Above all nothing green. No Limpopo smiles in this officers' mess, thank you very much. It's only women who insist on two veg. If women weren't around, there wouldn't be a man alive who'd eat broccoli. Or any of that finicky stuff, like rice with those little bits of red and yellow in, that make it look like someone else has eaten it first. Or *crudités* for God's sake. Certainly nothing glazed, or julienned, or drizzled; no sauce making its own tiny statement on a near-empty plate with five peas as garnish round the edge. And nothing

remotely resembling what caterers insist on calling so ghoulishly 'Finger Food'. Just good old-fashioned nursery food, like you used to get in the House of Lords.

That's what men say they like. But I've had the most delicious shooting lunches in England, and never cease to be amazed at those brilliant hostesses who cater so lavishly to shooting and non-shooting guests alike. Like one amazing day, lunching in a barn amongst the bales of straw, with the finest of damask table-cloths and polished silver, and baskets of the most wonderful fresh-baked assortments of breads and steaming cauldrons of *bouillabaisse*, and an old iron chandelier, candles lit, hanging from the rafters; or the warmth of a finer dining-room with comfort of a fire, and sturdy chairs, and shepherds' pie followed by treacle tart and clotted cream, lashings of wine, a huge cheese board and the port... who on earth could wish for anything more?

It was Colette who wrote that, if she had a son who was ready to marry, she would 'tell him to beware of girls who didn't like wine, truffles, cheese or music'. Clever woman. Food is an inherent part of the shooting scene too – the *only* reason, of course, why I seem to spend so much time droning on about it; and there is no finer sight for any shoot hostess than those lovely long ladened tables where everyone is in a haze of happiness, good food and Dow's, and where the only words you dread hearing are 'right everybody – five minutes please'...

As for stalking, any piece you take out on the hill (and we're speaking gastronomically here, you understand) is entirely a matter of personal preference. Probably Charles St. John got it right. Personally, and especially for hind-stalking in late December, I like to keep going with a slab of chocolate, and the thought of sweet tea laced with cloves and whisky once I'm back in the larder or the gun-room, followed by a deep peaty bath. And then only, a tray for two in front of the fire, with something delicious, and large stiff linen napkins and a magnum of best red for medicinal purposes, and hearing the storm howling outside... That's the very best *après-stalk* supper I can imagine.

Fun and Games with Men in Skirts

———◆———

nyone's first experience of a Highland Games is, I imagine, much like anyone's first experience of sex – everything's fairly chaotic, a lot of stuff happens that nobody's warned you about, it's very easy to lose the plot, you're faced with a lot of strangely terrifying things you've never been faced with before, and actually it's not that much fun. Added to which if you're female, by the end you're all done in and your hair's mussed. And the noise, my dear – indescribable – all those wheezing pipes, the groaning and yelling – you know what I mean.

The first time I ever attended a Highland Gathering, as it is also known – as in 'the gathering of the clans'- was many summers ago in Argyll. Although assuming that it was going to be just a Scottish version of any country fair in the south, I'd nevertheless, and luckily, made enquiries as what a lady novice should *wear*, at least, for such an occasion, so as not to frighten the horses. Following strict injunctions I therefore turned up carefully attired so as to be tidy ('no jeans, no scruff order or you'll be turned away from the Enclosure'... dear heaven – imagine the *shame...*) but un-remarkable, in a nice loden skirt and a good tweed jacket and with an umbrella stashed out of sight in a large handbag. Which was, luckily, perfect. I only mention these little sartorial details in case there is anyone left out there, someone perhaps from Siberia, Mars or the colonies, whose ignorance of Scottish rituals might, conceivably, be even greater than mine had been, and thus could possibly land them in the mire. In the event, it was a revelation.

Just before 10am, several hundred souls, all in Highland kit, congregated in the little town square for the traditional march up to the 'gathering field' a mile or so out of town. They would march behind the clan chiefs, all with eagle-feathers in their bonnets so they could be easily distinguished in battle of course, and the street-wide, serried ranks of pipers striding out ahead and leading the march. Not a pipe-band, mind you, but two or three hundred individuals who had all travelled here from the length and breath of the kingdom to play, and compete for the piping prizes, at the Games. As the town hall clock struck the hour, the march, and the pipes, began. The noise was, indeed, indescribable. After the first few minutes, however, having realised that everyone was in fact playing the same tune – well, more or less – you too began, almost unconsciously, to march in step... It conjured up all the old images – wars, passions, *Braveheart* and Young Lochinvar, raiding parties and skirmishes, clans and tribes joining together to rout, or celebrate, or dance, or mourn, or simply (remembering that fine romantic figure – the lone piper in the mist at dawn) to make music – the pipe-tassels and kilts swaying as if alive... And, suddenly, finding yourself caught up in all these engulfing emotions became heart-bursting and exhilarating.

This rapidly vanished once the gathering field hove into sight. The pipes whined to an unorchestrated halt, the march broke step and the rain started with gusto. We went in through the entrance gates, and there lay the empty field.

As the hours passed, of course, the place duly filled up. By mid-morning everything was in full swing. The hullabaloo was astonishing. The dancers, accompanied by pipes, were doing their neat twirly stuff on small square platforms – small bouncy girls, mostly Canadian, and men leaping over crossed swords; there were other pipers marching back and forth, being judged for individual performances by unseen judges skulking in small tents; there were relay runners and scores of children competing in unruly races around the field, being shouted at in stentorian west coast accents by red-faced organisers with loudspeakers; there were huge bare-chested caber-tossers in the middle of the field, yelling and groaning, and all the tug-of-war teams vociferously psyching themselves up along the edges. The locals had gathered up the far end together with ferret-fanciers, keepers in their tweeds, lurcher-breeders and the local talent, plus gaggles of tourists in raincoats, to mingle about the heaving throngs near the coconut-shies, the ice-cream and the hot-dogs stalls and the air-rifle stands, all shouting bawdy encouragement both to the contestants on the field and each other, and taking 'a refraishment or tu' before settling down to serious discussion with the malts in the beer-tent.

At the opposite end by the entrance, following the time-honoured principle of separating sheep from goats, there was a large roped-off area of folding wooden chairs encompassing The Enclosure (and a portaloo) for dignitaries and 'the gentry'. Here the county's nobs – both sexes sporting tartans of astonishing diversity and hues – and the senior clansmen, all in their lovely old bonnets and plaids and all called Angus or Alasdair, striding about as only Scotsmen in good kilts, with good knees, who are certain of looking their very best, can do, languidly entertained each other (no rowdiness here, thank you) and their obviously 'foreign' guests. Anyone, by the way, from south of the border, whatever their title, is considered foreign; and no foreigner should ever wear tartan; likewise, if a person comes from another country, referred to as 'abroad', they should never wear anything remotely hinting at national dress, which is considered frightfully naff. Their bored children, and any complete idiot who didn't know better, went off to join in the races with the locals.

Just to ring the changes, every couple of hours a full pipe-band would march out into the field. Everything else would grind untidily to a halt while they struck up; they played, marched and countermarched, leopard skins dancing on the drums and kilts swinging in step, the brasses glinting and the pipes echoing off the hills around, the cognoscenti tapping their feet to the beat. Some local big-wig would step forward self-importantly and take the salute; then the games, the yelling and the chaos would resume once again. It was a mixture of Bedlam and *Brigadoon*, in spades.

Having eaten a rain-sodden bap and done my duty all round, by quite early in the afternoon I began to feel a little weak and needing a lie down *now* – as one does – so, in a defeatist fashion, I made my excuses and left for some R. & R. 'Ach fer Gawd's sake hen, away an' put yer feets up,' Murdo the porter said sympathetically as I fell up the hotel steps. 'Dammit, ye'll be needin all yer strength fer the ball tonight'. He was right about that, anyway. six am the following morning – all of us on our umpteenth wind, and totally out of our skulls on a heady mixture of orange juice and reels, *but unvanquished* – we were still trying to navigate a *Duke of Perth* on the harbour pier, to an audience of astonished seals...

There is, it has to be admitted, an indefinable magic about a Highland Gathering.

Power Lines

———◆———

There's been a lot of discussion lately about what is referred to as 'the empowerment of women'. Presumably this refers mostly to those really alarming females who manage to juggle time, lives, nannies, share indexes and men with such ease and aplomb; those committed breakfast-meeting, top-IQ types with low-tolerance thresholds and high-maintenance hair and beautifully-cut suits and a company car, who earn enough to make the World Debt look like pin-money, employ catering firms for business entertainment at home, and never get 'flu.

I've never yearned to be a Powerful Woman. (Possible exception, Eleonor of Aquitaine, 'by the wrath of God, Queen'- a figure I've always regarded as being rather like my mother, only more reasonable.) However, the combination of glamour, potency and lots of the ready is admittedly very appealing, especially for those of us who wake up each day worrying about the gas-bill and with hair that appears to have been shredded by wild dogs. The closest most of us can get to female empowerment is ripping out the plug during a rugger match. Or, come to think of it, being, for a few magical moments, as good at something – anything would do, really – as our male peers, and respected by them for it...

It had been a great day. The houseparty was happy and relaxed, the Scottish west coast working its usual mellifluous magic on a group of friends who always came up to play around then, taking in a spot of fishing, going on the odd foray for a roe, inspecting the distilleries, listening to the racing in the car in the rain; an easy party to run, undemanding and un-fussed. After a day in scruff order, black tie was the norm and everyone got down to enjoying themselves: a late dinner followed by malt tastings, bridge or scrabble, music, endless talk and nonsense, lots of noisy horseplay.

This evening was no exception. No-one seemed tired and in fact, as seems to happen fairly regularly, 4am had come and gone unnoticed. Having made it that far it seemed daft to go to bed. No-one suggested breakfast al fresco; this time it was 'Let's go and

DO something.' Three people decided to take a boat and some rods out onto the loch, quite a cunning plan as it involved much heated argument, and further liquid fortification over the fly-boxes, regarding which flies should be used. Someone called for a game of backgammon, another wanted to finish off the end of a decanter by the dwindling fire. The rest of us mulled over possible alternative options. What about taking some guns and shooting the old 78's up the back drive? Too anti-social really, at that sort of hour. Croquet in the half-light? The midges would be out the moment dawn broke, but a small group decided on braving it... The six of us left thought again. A roebuck – now there's an idea – fresh liver for breakfast for anyone who could face it... 'Right' I said firmly. 'I'll be stalker. We'll be back by seven.'

Actually this was quite brave as I'd never acted as stalker before, but they weren't to know that. As is only to be expected at that sort of hour everyone was frightfully enthusiastic in a glazed, discombobulated way, and absolutely no help at all. So I got the rifle out – they'd all shot with that particular rifle before, so there wouldn't be any problem there – remembered the ammunition, grabbed a couple of camouflage jackets for anyone who might feel sartorially disadvantaged stalking in a black tie, flung the binoculars over my neck, a shawl over my long dress and a gralloching knife into the cleavage, herded my little group into the old Land Rover and we set off. Once a head-girl, you never lose the knack, like falling off a log.

Dawn was just beginning to break. After ten minutes we were out on the glen road and making for the far end where I'd in fact seen a nice little buck, doing his early-morning rounds by the river, a couple of days before. As we got near the spot I turned the engine off as I'd watched the stalkers do, to coast silently down the slope and let the machine come to a stop by itself so the brakes wouldn't squeal. Good thinking – it was very quiet out there. Everyone was silent. Calm and exuding confidence, I methodically scanned the river banks through the binoculars, praying that I was going to be right. 'I know he's there' I whispered (the best stalkers *always* talk to their stalking party, it keeps them awake as well as informed). 'What? because that's his patch:

he comes up from the river into that field then makes his way over to those whinn bushes. Just wait a bit, you'll see...' The dawn-patrol midge flight, with that unerring sense of the unwanted, began making inroads through the splits in the canvas roof, causing a certain amount of shifting and muted swearing in the back. 'Ssshhh... Look, there he is.'

My heart started thumping, but, having mercifully produced the rabbit out of the hat, I was now in total control. 'Right, Charlie, you're on for this? Well then, put on the cammo jacket – great. Now listen, *when* I tell you to get out, do it QUIETLY, don't even close the door ok? Just keep WELL DOWN and we'll both crawl over to the ditch there and down it along to the bank there. But *slowly* – no rush. I'll take the rifle now and I'll hand it to you on the bank, loaded and with the safety on. THEN I'll tell you when. Let's go.' Both of us had slithered out of the vehicle before I suddenly remembered I'd still got my evening sling-backs on, so discarded them on the road. He followed me as we crawled silently across, along the ditch and from there, up onto the bank. He scrabbled up next to me, and took the rifle while I watched the buck through the glasses. 'You ready? Muzzle clear? Wait until he's broadside... ok; right, whenever you want.' It was a perfect shot. The buck fell instantly, and lay still in the long grass. We waited a minute or more, as you do to make sure, but it was fine. Then we got to our feet, gave a thumbs-up sign and the car erupted in cheers. Charlie grinned inanely, his bow-tie only slightly askew. 'Now, re-load, just in case; I've got the knife here, we'll go over to him.'

So, with a long evening dress tucked up into my knickers and in bare feet but with the earrings still in place, I strode off into the dew-ladened grass followed by an admiring audience; gralloched the beast to their obvious astonishment, and dragged it back with them to the road where I retrieved my shoes. 'COR, that was brilliant... didn't know you knew how to do all that – real pro. stuff... what a stalker eh Charlie? ... First time out with a woman hey?? Ho ho ho...' Talk about empowerment – I was so pleased with myself I could have burst.

Nemesis struck (natch) later that day. A very irate estate-manager took me to one side ('A word please ma'm') and gave me the biggest bollocking of my life. He'd been told what had happened

(we'd hung the beast up in the game-larder very properly of course) and just WHAT did I think I'd been doing, it was the most damned-fool thing ever, and me in my glad-rags too – what would have happened if the beast had been wounded, would I have gone running off after it over the march in my bare feet? HE was ultimately responsible for all sporting matters, not me, he didn't BELIEVE anyone could have been so stupid, and I would kindly never do anything like that again...

He was right of course, and I apologised fulsomely. But it had been the most wonderful moment.

The Knowledge

———◆———

We once engaged a French *au pair* for a couple of months one spring. It was not a huge success because we were in Scotland, it rained most of the time, and it also turned out she was pregnant. Every morning in the kitchen there would be these terrible groans as Lorelle appeared, in what barely passed for clothing, to help with breakfast. She'd take one look at the porridge, clutch her mouth and run, muttering '*excusez-moi*, aa sink aa weel be seek' and vanish for hours. She didn't do my small daughter's French much good – nor her English come to think of it. 'Mummy, Lorelle says she wants a shit. Oh, and pepper.' 'WHAT? Darling... oh never mind... Lorelle you simply CANNOT say things like that...' After a lengthy session of tears all round, it transpired of course that the poor girl merely wanted to write a letter home.

In spite of her proclivity to throw up at regular intervals, Lorelle's own grasp of the English language did however improve dramatically, as she went everywhere clutching a small notebook in which to record the more interesting linguistic idioms encountered during the day. She and the daughter would set off for, say, a visit to the farm, Lorelle clad invariably in a leather pelmet and spiky heels (not really a *country* gel you understand), where I would find them deep in conversation with the farmer, exploring the merits of 'a great big sappy sheep' or the more detailed facets of animal husbandry generally. 'See yon beastie there, wail, he'll still have the stones on him come October ah rekkun.' Lorelle, pen at the ready, was all attention: 'Ahhh... pliss, wat eees eeet, ze stones?' My daughter, who was at that tedious age when fascination with bodily parts and functions was at its zenith, would then give a vividly mimed translation, and the next minute Lorelle would, once again, be retching over a wall.

We learned quickly enough what would set her off. Pheasant chicks, catching mackerel, even shooting pigeons were ok, gutting a rabbit or gralloching a roe was not. A day on the river was fine, but cleaning a freshly-caught fish, or talking about the ingre-

dients for haggis, definitely wasn't. Even the dog getting rid of a hair-ball seemed to have the most fundamental effect on her. One way and another she seemed relieved to say goodbye at the end of the two months' stay.

Mind you, all that red-in-tooth-and-claw stuff does take a bit of getting used to if you're a stranger to it. Children are a great antidote to the squeamish. 'Oh and Jimmy's collie's going to have pups soon cause we saw her tied to the big black dog for – ooo – HOURS and we watched and Jimmy says it doesn't hurt a BIT...' Visitors blanch and sit quivering on the edge of the sofa; afterwards come the remonstrations: 'Darling, do you really think it's wise...' Of course it is. Any knowledge you can acquire at any time is a Good Thing.

Take a line of guns, for instance, any Saturday in winter in the Home Counties; it would be interesting to wonder how many of them could set a vermin trap, or make up a line of sewelling, or indeed think that an eco-pile is anything other than a painful ailment you get as a member of Greenpeace. I'm not suggesting that a course of game-management is a pre-requisite for enjoying the odd day's shooting, but we all need all the help we can get.

And the earlier it's acquired the better. The fact that every female child, from the age of four months, instinctively *knows* how to flirt with the opposite sex, may be a genetic safety switch: but a girl will also go on gaining Vital Knowledge of a multitude of things which will affect her, throughout her life. Like the fact that, for instance, there are four things you simply never criticise in a man (how he drives, shoots, makes love or cocktails); she will also learn that she will be expected not only to read and use both a map and the FT index, but also that she will have to converse knowledgeably about military terminology, interest rates and cricket scores, *and* understand that Real Men don't fold socks. A man for his part will (hopefully) have learned, and therefore will know (1) how to pick his clothes up off the floor; (2) that it is never permissible, or wise, to keep any girl waiting and (3) that he should never either question her intelligence or her silhouette ('putting on a little weight are we?' is *absolutely* the wrong approach) or hassle her when they are already thirty minutes late for an engagement and she is still flinging things around the bedroom like some psychotic gerbil and wailing that she's got nothing to wear.

As a girl, you will also learn 'outdoors' stuff like sports, driving etc., and usually by being taught by a man. Men are very good instructors. But just make sure you're not being taught by a man whom you *know*, like a father, brother or boyfriend, otherwise it'll turn into one of those 'No no NO, not like THAT, BRAKE dammit, Christ didn't you SEE that bicyclist... aaaaarghhhhh...' sagas, and you end up fighting like cats. Likewise, being taught to shoot by one of your nearest and dearest should be avoided *at all costs.* 'For God's sake woman don't just stand there WAVING the thing round, get it properly into your shoulder, there. And uncross your legs for heaven's sake... what? well I can't help that – now stop mucking about and get ON with it'; or the real killer: 'O for the love of Mike... why not shoot where it's *going* rather than where it's *been?*' which inevitably leads to tears before bedtime.

Most of this sort of practical knowledge is, unquestionably, best imparted by professionals. And later, when you have managed to bring down the highest partridge of the day, and the whole line of men is purring round you afterwards and saying 'BLOODY good shot that' and asking for your telephone number, you can blush sweetly and disclaim any talent of your own, putting it down to 'a really brilliant man who taught me'. That'll cheer them up no end.

On second thoughts, don't bother – they'll have assumed it anyway.

Judge Not

(or: Who laughs last, laughs last)

H aving people to stay in Scotland is lovely. The only house rule is No Dogs Indoors as the family dogs – models of all that is best in canine manners – become upset and then it all goes pear-shaped.

Several years ago, a friend arrived to stay with a large blonde labrador bitch called Jura for a week's walking up grouse. First day out, and every ten minutes the line of guns, keepers, participants and camp followers would have to grind to a halt as the dog took off, yet again, hot on the trail: hares and pippets, snipe, shadows and rabbits – anything that moved, streaking like an arrow across the hills in a cloud of heather bloom... 'Jura WILL you come here...' he would scream repeatedly, while the rest of the line stood about, making silly comments like '*num or nonne*, would that be?' and giggling, waiting to see what would happen. He would then belabour her furiously, and contrary to what the manuals tell you to do, once she had finally deigned to return. The keeper came wandering up in a casual manner and watched with interest. Finally he shook his head. 'Och it's too late fer tha' surr. Yeeers an' yeeers too late I'd say...'

This went on for a week. The *finale* came one evening when Jura couldn't be found. We all searched and screeched and yelled, inside and out, but to no avail. I returned indoors to get away from the midges. The study door was open; there, reclining at her ease like Madame Recamier in a large pale old leather chair, was Jura. She looked at me a trifle shiftily, then smiled and peed. Not just a dribble, mind you – it was an absolute flood – voluminous, steaming, and interminable, and all over the leather. I stomped off in a rage to find her owner and inform him, through clenched teeth, that his damned dog had materialised, and pointed him in the direction of the study. When he saw what had happened, there was no shock-horror – no apology. Merely a plaintive: 'Oh Jura, how COULD you?' The resulting immovable stain was thereafter known, rather unoriginally, as the bitch's revenge.

We had a rather senior judge to stay one year. He had made it abundantly clear that, although he much looked forward to being with us, his *real* reason for coming was that he wanted to fish. No stalking or shooting thank you, picnics and so forth would be fine but – um – how was the river right now? What was it likely to be like during his visit? He would arrive on the early plane, perhaps he could just stop and look on the way back to the house, you just never knew with these spate rivers did you and it would be such a pity to miss even half a chance … Yes *yes*, I reassured him, don't WORRY, do whatever you like, someone will meet you off the plane, see you when we see you. The artist and the Scotsman, perfect and amenable co-house-guests, volunteered to look after him.

It transpired afterwards that they did a magnificent job. The judge had his fishing bag over his shoulder, plus waders in a plastic bag in one hand and rod in the other, as he hurried off the plane. He had to be forcibly restrained from climbing into the car and driving off and was made to wait for his luggage. Finally, after a lot of genial gossip and general procrastination, the two others joined him in the car. They insisted that he sat in the back – 'more comfortable really' – and set off, driving rather slowly and with exaggerated care so as, they assured him, to ensure 'not hitting any stray sheep'.

The judge proceeded to describe to them at length some of the fish he had caught recently, most of the fish he had caught over the past few years, all of the fish he hoped to catch in the fairly immediate future; the size of fly he'd used, the types of fly he had brought with him in his fly-box, the length and weight of the rod he had with him at this very moment, why he had chosen it rather than one of his many others, on and on, *usque ad nauseam*... The

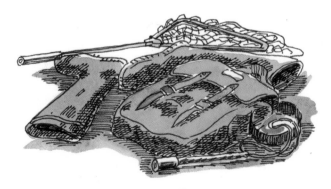

two in the front listened aimiably.

Suddenly the Scotsman, who was driving, slowed down even further and brought the car to a rest on the top of a small bump, flanked by a couple of old bits of iron railing which served as a timely indication to passing motorists that they should refrain from driving off the road at this particular point. It was in fact a bridge, over a very narrow trickle of brackish water which oozed out from an unkempt field of thistles and whinn bushes on one side of the road, and away into some heavy rushes and scrubland on the other. A group of cows, belly-deep in undergrowth, stopped munching and stared at them mournfully. The Scotsman turned off the engine, and looked at the artist. 'It's looking good today, isn't it' he said, quietly. The artist, a fine fisherman himself (this had been casually referred to earlier on) nodded and, winding down the window on his side, peered out through the old iron railing decorated with baler twine and the odd sheep hairs, and carefully appraised the pathetic dribble seeping, almost invisible, through the tangle of weeds and nettles below. 'You're right 'he replied at length. 'Just perfect – let's see...just a bit overcast, not too bright – which way's the wind? – ah yes... anything happening your side?' They managed to keep up this nonsense for some time.

The judge was totally nonplussed. 'Er... are you sure this is it?' he finally asked, somewhat anxiously; 'this is nothing like the size of river I'd imagined...' 'Good heavens man' cried the Scotsman, apparently losing all patience, 'can ye no recognise a fine bit of spate when ye see it? By jinks, some folks are hard to please; and since we've been hearing all about yer prowess with a rod ye'd better get yerself out and into yer wee wellies right now, and let's see some action... Hang on a minute though, is that not a rise...?' 'Yes, yes indeed' the artist agreed immediately; ' I'm sure I saw something move just there... back-cast's a bit tricky of course but – I dunno – worth a try I'd say – no real sport if it's too easy, eh? Now, do watch out for that half-sunken bit of ironmongery by the bushes ... oh and it's a tad uneven beyond the cowpats... but don't worry, you'll be fine.'

It was only once they had actually persuaded the judge to get out of the car and take a proper look that they reckoned they'd won. But in the end the judge had the last laugh. Next day, he managed to convince the artist that he'd seen a monstrous rise out in the middle of a loch, and offered to row him out to it, and the artist, after some beautiful casting, brought in a four-inch rudd. When they arrived back at the house, the judge was still chortling.

'What?' we all cried, 'you, the famous fisherman, and all you can catch is a four-inch RUDD?'

'Ah yes, but you know, four inches is big for a rudd' replied the artist, crossly.

A Long Shot

Why is it we all enjoy making things as difficult as possible – a secret desire to be tested, to overcome? But then difficulty breeds excellence – the challenge is all. And heroes are those who accept – and sometimes create – the challenge, whatever it may be. To encircle the globe in a boat or a balloon, to run the fastest mile, to 'reach the unreachable stars...' how daft, but how splendid. My personal hero, the first man to eat a snail, goes unsung in the lists.

Shooting is all about challenges: you pick the highest bird, take the longest shot, down the most clays, make the smallest group at the greatest distance. 'And it's not for the sake of a ribboned coat, or the selfish hope of a season's fame'; not all shooting exploits have the public award of silver pots, or the Queen's prize-winner's chair. Most indeed are private achievements – simply to shoot better than you believe you can. Shooting birds on the wing, the concept of 'Shooting Flying', was the most difficult, challenging and 'sporting' of shots. It was probably first tried in the late 1600s, when the plate of an engraving of that name appeared in Richard Brome's *Gentleman's Recreation*. The very nature of the weapon, the delay in igniting the charge, the cumbersome muzzle-loader itself, all added to the difficulties of the sportsman; not to mention the fact that, in the Brome engraving, they are also shooting from horseback...

We were talking about the concept of the sporting shot, and my daughter told me a story she had heard whilst shooting in Africa. Apparently a group of Englishmen had gone out on a week-long hunting safari and, much taken with both the ability and the charm of their Professional Hunter, had invited him to visit them the following season and stalk in Scotland.

He duly arrived. The first day out, having been properly briefed and, as is customary whether you are shooting beasts in Africa or Aberdeenshire, having been made to shoot the regulation group at a paper target to everyone's satisfaction the party, consisting of the P.H., his host and Hamish the stalker, set off up the hill. It was a perfect day, sunny with the odd helpful cloud and a nice breeze, ideal. The only minor problem was the flies which were obviously bothering the beasts and keeping them on the move; but at least the stags were there, in quantity, and the party spied happily, and walked, and spied, and talked, for several hours.

Finally, a large herd of stags was seen. The party crawled in as far as they could but could get no closer than about 500 yards away from the beasts, who were not lying down but feeding – a step or two, tossing their heads to get rid of the flies, another step or two. The three of them huddled in behind a rock to discuss the problem. Since, as Hamish had put it, 'they're fair jittery today' it was agreed that, instead of following in behind the stalker to take up a position for a shot, the P.H. should go in on his own, 'yez bein' a stalker yerself, as one might say, sor'. No problem. The selected stag had been clearly identified and agreed on – an old beast with long back points at the top, very dark from a session in the peat hags – and the P.H. was, after all, a very experienced and good shot. The rifle was loaded up and, quite properly, for a long crawl, returned to its slip, the P.H. set off on his belly like a snake, and the other two took up their binoculars to watch.

Five hundred yards, give or take, on your belly, navigating

hills, lochs and burns and peat hags and waiting for the odd cloud to give you cover when you're slithering across the open patches, is time-consuming. The stags were still moving and feeding and unaware, and the P.H. was doing brilliantly and had got extremely close... too close in fact, dammit, hadn't he seen the beasts move towards him while he'd been clambering out of that last bit of burn? For, suddenly, they were there, no more than 50 yards away from him...A struggle with the leather slip to get the rifle out – pulling back the bolt as he got steady and, without warning, a shot goes off. What on earth had happened?

The herd, not unnaturally, bolted. No hanging around, no stopping after a bit to look back, they just took off – the big old dark stag with the long back points going for his life and well out in front. And, to the watchers' amazement, there was the P.H. on his feet, the rifle up in his shoulder, and the herd by now flying away over the hills – a good 350 to 400 yards out by now and still galloping hard and ('he's never going to try from there, och fer God's sake...') a shot; and the big old dark stag with the long back points, way out in front of his herd, drops like a stone.

By the time that the host and the stalker finally got up to the dead stag (a perfect, textbook shot, even though taken from the most horrible angle), the P.H., who had got there in half the time and had already and most professionally gralloched the beast, was sitting waiting for them. He was clearly extremely upset. Shaking his head he started to try and explain that, look, he was terribly sorry, look, the safety catch slipped as he was getting ready to fire, he hoped it was ok to have taken that second shot like that without checking with Hamish, it was such a terrible accident to have done that with the safety, look, and I'm just really so very very sorry man...

According to the host's later report, Hamish clapped him on the shoulder. 'Stop all yer gabbin' will ya, and jus' listen' he said firmly. 'Ah've never seen such a sportin' shot in all ma days, nor such a fine one neither, an' tha's a farct. *An* ye've done all ma durrty work for me as wail. Come awa now, we got a puckle o' drinkin' to do down at the larder once we've got this beast on the back o' the pony.' Which they did.

De Rerum Naturum

———◆———

Compared to the Continentals, we're very lax in this country when it comes to knowledge about our surroundings, especially as far as shooting or stalking is concerned. As long as you can shoot safely and straight you can, simply, go out and shoot. But in Norway for instance, or Germany or Austria, it is mandatory to pass various levels of written and practical exams in order to carry and use a firearm. You are required to be able to differentiate all the animal tracks and bird calls, recognise the different type of damage done to flora by different varieties of game, and to know the life-cycle and eating habits of every species. You must be able to differentiate between different calibres of shot and of bullet, know the velocities and physical properties of the various types of ammunition and also be able to assess, by forensically examining a wound, by which calibre of ammunition it was inflicted. You must be able to despatch, clean and butcher a beast properly, and therefore you must know each species of game literally inside out.

And, faced with a target at a hundred meters under approved supervision, you must be able to shoot a group of the required diameter and in three positions – standing, shooting and kneeling. After you have satisfied the authorities of your abilities on all these counts you are then awarded a certificate to prove your fitness to shoot and hunt. And you will also have to be able to recognise every species of the flora, as well as knowing the properties of all plants, trees and vegetation, in the area in which you intend to hunt.

Here, not. The only shooting ability needed to stalk, for instance, is that of being able to put three or four rounds more or less together on a target and that's it. The stalker or keeper will be there to tell you everything else and will gralloch the beast at the end. As for habitat we are (well, I am) pig-ignorant. Something like the 18th century Irish duelling codes, or Egyptian history of the first pharaonic period or the alignment of the zodiac, I can do that; but ask me the name of a plant and I'm a goner. (I don't think I'm absolutely alone here: a friend once confessed that she thought that *gypsophila* was a fear of vagrants.)

Hence something perfectly normal like a nice early-morning roe stalk turns into a display of ignorance that our Continental friends wouldn't credit. You're huddled down with the stalker, spying through the binoculars over towards the burn which, he's assured you, is the territory of a particularly desirable old buck. 'Tha's him, behind that scrubby bit on the far side, ah'm thinkin'...' 'Where? All I've got is a lump of brown stuff, behind the two stones... see where the bare branches of that woody red tree stick out?' 'Ach no, ah'm lookin' further down... see yon yellow bit where the fence runs into into the water by them dark bushes...?' 'Still nothing... hang on though, you see the square patch of green by the fence? Well, go right and you hit the bottom of the thingummy tree, the one with the funny top. Then go up to two o'clock and there's that orangey clump and the dead branch of whateveritis hanging down, there's something moving behind the scrub, what is it, damn, my binos have misted up...' '...Aye, ah'm with ya now... Yon's a sheep, mum.'

I was totally humbled one day when Donald and I took out a tenant, a passionate botanist, for another roe stalk. 'Ah YES,' I could hear him mutter behind me as we all crawled down a narrow ride in one of the plantations. 'Lesser twayblade AND creeping lady, good...' I thought he was just being gratuitously personal but didn't comment. Then he grabbed a moment to ask about what sounded like pinus preloxera and something-sexiflora and finally, in the middle of a rather tricky manoeuvre – trying to negotiate on our bellies under the fence without making the wire twang – came a joyful whisper. 'Heavens, it can't be... yes it is... *Arctostofalus urvi ursi*, well I'll be damned...'

Donald, not a man to be duly overwhelmed even by a Sublime Prince of the Royal Secret, turned and suggested innocently that, as to his certain knowledge the roe wouldn't give a bugger about fancy names, perhaps the gentleman would prefer to stay right there and make notes rather than continue with the stalk?

I'm not knocking it mind you: I'm dead impressed by erudition; but I guess we all occasionally give the wrong impression, quite unintentionally, by simply *assuming* that the other person knows exactly what we're talking about... It happened only last September when a girl friend of mine, having shot – for the first time ever – quite beautifully and consistently at the target, was persuaded by us all that she ought to go out on the hill with Donald the next day and try for a stag.

Determined to leave nothing to chance, I thought I'd given her the fullest possible briefing on what to expect: what she'd have to do, what she should wear, footwear most important, and just take a bit of chocolate and a bap perhaps out of the 'piece' box and leave the rest in the vehicle for afterwards, lots of fresh-water springs on the hill if you get thirsty; don't worry about keeping up, Donald will only walk at your pace and you walk right close up behind him; and as for the shot, just go up the back of the front leg and another handspan above (so she knew exactly where to aim) oh and take a stick, third leg and all that... the works. They set off the following morning in Donald's van, he was making her laugh about something as he always did, he'd take care of her beautifully...

According to her version later on, they'd driven as far as the glen road when they came across a bunch of cows munching this-tles on the verge; at which point she summoned up all her courage and asked him if he wouldn't mind stopping the car a moment to explain something about which she wasn't *absolutely* certain, *would* he mind, *sorry* to be so stupid...

Thus it was that, in the middle of the road and surrounded by a herd of interested cattle, Donald gave an anatomy lesson with the aid of his stalking stick. 'Now if ya just go up HERE – och stand still ya bitch – and then up a bitty more round HERE, that's where the heart'll be ... aye, it'll be exactly the same on the other side... An' the liver's about THERE, and the lungs is here – mind out, don't step... ach well never mind, an' there's me just washed ma van out too...'

All he told us afterwards was that 'she shot like she'd bin doin' it all her life – heart-shot nae problem – a fine wee wifey.'

A Switch in Time

Stalking on one of those lovely wild estates up the west coast, we were just setting out when the keeper, stopping, asked which way I would prefer to go up the hill: 'the easy way or the hard?'. One glance at what looked like Chomolungma rearing ahead of us and I opted for the first. Silly me. Having trudged wearily behind him up a track with a gradient of 1 in 4 with no break for *three hours*, I collapsed sobbing at the top, and prayed that death would come as a friend. A long time passed, of which I remember nothing except wondering vaguely if my will was in order, while he kindly and silently spied for non-existent beasts in the distance. Finally, slowly, life ebbed back: 'So...ogod...what's the... hard way then?...' He laughed and lit a cigarette. 'Well, jus' straight up the rock-face yonder – och it's no' so hard, an' it's a damned sight faster... we'll go down tha' way later.' We did too. I don't know which was worse. I don't normally go in for abseiling without a rope, but it taught me a lesson I've never forgotten: given the option, you *always* take the hard way up, and the easy way down.

The fact that I'd been almost beaten by a hill was made even more galling when I remembered that this had been the very same estate on which Fraser Darling, that passionate sportsman, had stalked barefoot during the summer of 1935; perhaps even where he wrote about his beloved sport... Well, that's the way it goes. But to think that, having always rather romantically envisaged myself as a latter-day Marchioness of Breadalbane, swirling round the high hills as a very old lady; or indeed as another Horatio Ross, the celebrated athlete and prize-winning rifle shot – he shot in the Scottish Eight for many years – who first took Fealar, the highest-standing lodge in the kingdom, in 1828, and was still stalking the grounds at the age of eighty; and here was I, in my prime and a total wreck.

Mind you, being an athlete or winning prizes at Bisley does not *necessarily* make you a good stalking shot. A friend of ours, shooting his match-rifle in the back position – a stance that the Americans, with unconscious wit, call 'seemyfeetal'- has won, over the years, more gold and silver than anyone in living memory. His stalking experience has consisted of a total of three outings. On both of the first two occasions he was asked to shoot two beasts in succession, which he did. However on neither occasion were either of the beasts that fell dead – each with a perfect shot to the base of the neck – the ones he had been aiming at. As amazing luck would have it, however, on both occasions the fallen beasts were pronounced by the stalker to be so old, and in such bad condition, as to not be worth recovering; so, although no-one could work out quite how it had happened, mercifully all turned out well enough in the end.

The third time he went out on the hill was one blustery day at home, and we were given a full report later that evening by the stalker. Duncan, who knew all about both his charge's reputation as a prize-winning shot and his previous rather hairy experiences on the hill, had kept well clear of any herds – which he reckoned was just asking for trouble – and had searched for a single beast away on its own. Finally he'd spied a switch, standing alone and broadside on, some 180 yards out. The story continued as follows: 'The mannie was fine – no' out o' breath an' pairfectly calm – an' he'd had a fair wee time gettin' himself comfortable-like before linin' up for the sho'. Are ye right now sor, sez I, an' he sez yes. Take yer time sez I – there's no hurry, he's no seein' us. So I hear him breathe in and out, nice an' easy, then a wee squeeze an' bang, the sho' goes off. Nothin'. Damn beast just stands there. No matter, just re-load sor, sez I. Bang again; nothin'. An' again, an' still nothin'. Christ, I didn'a know wha' to do, I can tell ye, and there wuz a fair bit swearin' goin' on but I thought wail, what the hail; so I sez to him quiet-like, No bother sor, yous just carry on, we've got all day yet'.

Apparently five more shots were fired, each to no effect, the stag merely gazing about and feeding, totally unperturbed. 'Mebbe it was the wind, that the beast didna hear the shots, or mebbe it was deaf, or just plain stupid fer God's sake... but here am I dolin' out the cartridges like they was sweeties when the mannie shouts an oath, jumps to his feet, lies down again but on his back with the rifle through his knees, and shoots the thing stone dead.'

Duncan took off his cap and shook his head. 'I'll be damned. So I sez to him, Tha's a bloody fine sho', sor, an' no' afore time if ye don't mind my sayin' so... An' then the poor soul's apologising, an' blethering on how he's more used to shootin' tha' way round... Is tha' a farct? sez I. In tha' case why in hell didya no' say airlier, ya bugger – we'duv saved werselves a puckle ammunition if ya had.'

Grousing Again

T he Editor-in-Chief rang me one day and, having asked very correctly about my health, put it to me – quite firmly, I thought, for an early morning call – that I might like to write about being in a grouse-butt, and in time for the evening post, said TTFN and put the phone down.

I cannot describe how my heart fell at this order from Him Upstairs. A jilted *fiancée*, told to describe her ideal honeymoon, could not have felt less happy at the prospect. For the fact is that, although everyone dreams of being invited to shoot driven grouse, few are called, and I'm not one of them.

As far as a woman is concerned, you can be asked to shoot any variety of game in this country – intergalatic pheasants or fast partridges; pigeon or geese in gales; snipe or woodcock in the Western Isles; wild, or even reared, duck (if you really like that sort of thing) – as well as any amount of game in other countries. But I have a theory that the only women to be invited to shoot driven grouse are those who already have their own. As an ordinary, average lady-shot, you're probably more likely to be asked to join the SEALS than to shoot driven grouse.

This however is not to say that you cannot be asked to stand in a grouse-butt behind a male gun and enjoy the day. The first time I was ever invited up to Scotland for the Twelfth, an innocent girl of 20-something with no experience of such things, but heart a-flutter, and bidden by a young man who not only possessed his own grouse moor, but whose tweed was of so totally delectable a

hue of dusty pink that I'd already made up my mind to marry him just for the sake of it. I was properly equipped with what I had been assured was the 'correct kit' for the occasion – pretty brogues with tassels on the lace-up tongues, fine delicately-coloured shooting stockings, a tweed jacket, a divided skirt, a fetching blouse with a scarf at the neck and exactly the right, rather feminine, shooting hat. (This was of course in the Middle Ages – nowadays girls just wear jeans.) I arrived the night before by train.

Next morning was fine, but quite suddenly and unexpectedly, two hours after we'd set out, the temperature plummeted, the winds got up from Siberia and the heavens opened. I spent the ensuing day huddled down in the bottom of the butts in thick mud, soaked to the skin, chilled to the marrow, deafened and battered by ejecting cartridges, trodden underfoot by the *bloody* young man who was dancing about in his *bloody* pink tweed saying things like Hurry Up For God's Sake Willy and Haaar, Christ What A Shot – and then stepped on my ankle *and broke it* – plus the loader and three large dogs, and being sworn at profusely for getting in the way. I looked like a traffic accident and the dogs had savaged the hat. I tell you, it was worse than sailing. Moral: check the weather forecast before accepting invitations of an unknown nature anywhere and, if it's not going to be good, break your *own* leg at home, it's much simpler.

Some years later, married to someone else and with more *savoire faire*, I stood with my husband in the properly lined grouse-butts of North Wales. It was a grand day. I'd learned what to take: plus-twos, a long-sleeved cotton shirt, an old shooting cap of my father-in-law's and ear-defenders, plus a (discreet) paperback, a heavy sweater and a thin mackintosh jacket rolled up in an old game bag. I was as happy as a clam sitting at the back of the butt on my nice tripod stick during the drives, musing about grouse generally (why are grouse better than men? Because in their case (1) 'thick and fast' are adverbs, not adjectives; (2) you can pick them up and not wonder where they've been before; (3) when you get one, you're not committed to a lifetime of washing its socks etc. etc.), talking to the dogs, making appreciative noises and keeping well clear of feet, loaders, empty cartridges and invectives. There were lots of chums and masses of birds; the sun shone, it was all divine.

Towards the end of the last drive of the day, we're on the end of the line and my husband gets something in his eye. A fly, a bit of heather, a passing blonde, I don't know what it was but panic stations ensued. 'I can't see... arggghhh... NO, I mean I CAN'T SEE dammit ... here, take my gun... no don't just TAKE it woman, take it and SHOOT for God's sake... of course you can, you've had lessons haven't you... just take the thing and GET ON WITH IT...we're on the end, with luck you won't have to fire...' A shooting veteran (two whole hours at shooting school), I took the gun and loaded it. It weighed a ton and, moreover, had a cast like a mule. I stood in the approved Stanbury position, waited for what seemed like for ever, and finally caught sight of something flying in at speed. I remember thinking that I hadn't realised grouse were so small, closed my eyes and fired. I looked up again, and it wasn't there. 'GOT IT' I screamed in delight. Nothing else came near me.

At the end of the drive the loader marched out some 20 yards in front, cast about diligently in the heather and finally bent to pick up something. 'Yours I think, madam' he said, solemnly turning and handing me my trophy. It was a very large, dead, bumblebee.

Notes from Scotland

Isn't it strange how people have suspicious minds? Politicians, policemen and wives probably need to, but in the main, folk are generally fairly uncomplicated and fairly prosaic about life. Granted, there are some of us who don't have a suspicious bone in our body but who are, well, just a bit *wary* – on guard, as it were, against the worst-case scenario. Nothing wrong with that, it's like keeping your fingers crossed, a perfectly logical form of insurance and of being prepared, like Mrs. Hennypenny lying on her back with her feet in the air in case the sky fell down; and it means that when it all turns out ok at the end, well, it's better than Christmas. I don't really like surprises myself (like when they give you a surprise party, and you're always the one wearing the wrong thing...). But the truly suspicious mind is always looking for the hidden agenda, the maggot in the lettuce. It was said that Talleyrand, on being told that Czar Alexander would not, after all, be attending a conference because he was dead, replied thoughtfully 'Ahhh, but I wonder what the *real* reason is?'

The Scots are like this. A grudging, sour, crabbity lot they can be. (It was a Scotsman after all who complained, when they'd dealt him all the trumps, that 'a lot of them were small'.) You can say something uncontroversial like Nice Day Isn't It and they answer 'Mebbe' or 'Is tha' a farct?' or 'Wail, ahm no' so sure'. Always weighing it up, putting it in the balance against the greater scheme of things. Guy canny. But as many a visitor to these northern parts has discovered, the Scots cannot be dismissed as merely a bunch of gloomy psychotics. No: it's really that they don't suffer fools gladly, and are never afraid to say so.

One evening everyone was gathered in the village hostelry for a farmers' dinner. One of the senior grieves was heard to say proudly that he'd had a hundred percent lambing that year. 'Ach awaywiddyaboyo' broke in a surly fellow, one of the less popular members of the community, wearing what is known as 'a farctor's soot' and clearly well under the influence of the local hooch. 'Tha's fer the tuth fairy. How could yew be havin' *wanhanredprecent* lambin', *an yew wid only eighty sheep?*' The room exploded in laughter. 'Oho' came a delighted voice from the back. 'Wait till yur boss is hearin tha' Sandy – it'll be afta the Busynes School fer yew, ya great puddinheid … Purrasoakinnit an git yer brain in geer, mon.'

I went out stalking hinds one early December with Old Rae, a small wizened Glaswegian of advanced years, unrelenting Eeyore-like gloom and the face of a manic-depressive ant. It was bitterly cold and with horizontal sleet and as we started up the hill the mist came down. After two hours of climbing and now chilled almost numb, we came round the side of a corrie. Old Rae stopped dead and I bumped straight into him as I'd been keeping my head well down. 'There y'ar' he announced, as if he'd just pulled off a particularly spectacular conjuring trick. 'Three hinds needin' shot. An yizzle goanmissem all, nae doot.' Filled with foreboding, I got ready, peering through the scope at three small ghosts looming in and out of the whiteness. I fired at the first one and, luckily (it was not a day to go running round the hill looking for anything wounded), missed her clean. 'Hah, ye silly bitch, ye went right over its bluddy arse' Old Rae muttered, a shade triumphantly I thought. 'Try aginan' fergoadsake duit proper.' 'No, I can't even see through the 'scope with this mist, I'm not going to try again' I said crossly. 'Och furraluvapete' came the reply; 'thasa bliddy fine start tae the day then.'

Later on, I managed to pull off a tricky shot at a beast lying

facing away from us behind a rock, with only the top of her head showing. 'Wailnoo, I dinna ken whirrahel yes wuz aimina', ya cuduv missed her easy…' 'But Rae, you told me to take the shot.' 'Aye, bu'ah naivair reckoned yed hi'er.' Such positive vibes already. It was a Wee Free minister who was reputed to have said

that he knew Christ had turned the water into wine but he 'didna think anny the bitter of Him forrit'.

But I mind well (as they say) the times without number of sheer delight, the daft moments, the funny stories, the disasters always redeemed by a sense of the ridiculous. The time the handyman, who was colour-blind, painted my father-in-law's desk bright red 'but arterall, it did say Vernish on the wee tin'. The time the Frenchman shot a blackbird, later smuggled into the kitchen by the keeper and produced, with a flourish and from under a huge silver dish-cover, by the cook at dinner. The time the ferrets got up Old Rae's leggings; and the memorable day when one of the shooting tenants, a brute of a man who had tried Donald's patience to the limit, finally shot a stag...

He was a hopeless shot. Beasts would take off with splintered ankles, bullets would whizz round the hill and ricochet off rocks – days out with him were one that no-one looked forward to and the two stalkers would be found huddled in a corner every morning flipping a coin... 'Ye'd set off well enough' Donald explained, 'hopin' the mannie'd finally fire one decent sho' in his life. An' aivry evenin' ye'd come back knackered out yer skull, havin' run miles arter some puir wounded beast. An' himself, ach he wasnae bothered, jus' complainin' arter everything. Ah've seen maself wavin' ma bluddy handkerchief a' a stag afore now, when ah didna feel upta peltin' o'er the hills furtherest o' the day. Bluddy toerag.'

I was in the house the day in question. A scrunch of tyres by the back door and in he strides, flinging off his boots and hollering for attention, very pleased with himself. A base-of-the-neck shot at, oh, extreme range, how about that then, stag dead in his tracks, stalker couldn't have anything to complain about this time eh?

I took some whisky up to the larder where Donald and the pony-boy were hauling the carcass off the weighing chains amidst the usual chatter. The bottle was passed round and Donald continued his account of the day's action. 'He'd clean missed two beasts airlier on, an' then all of a sudden there was this stag, no' ninety yards out an' broadside on – pairfect. Feedin' quietly, a wee step forwurd now an' then, nae bother. So wunce agin ah says to the man, Right sor, take 'im now, nice an'easy – shakin' like a terrier he wuz. An then ah think to maself, hang on – yon's a fairish young beast an' far too good fer this goon ta wound, so with a bit o' luck he'll miss him, an' that'd be jus fine. But ah can feel him holdin' his breath fer the shot and then damme, just as he lets it go, the stag only takes a pace forrard and walks slam into it... ah couldna believe ma eyes. Stone deid tu, buggerit. If he'd only just stood still, the mannie'd have missed him clean six inches in front, and the stupid crittur goes and steps straight out into the bluddy bullet...' Donald shook his head sadly. 'Ah naivair saw a pur wee beast had such effin' bad luck. Fair vexed ah wuz ah can tell ye. *Slainte.*'

We drank, to the stag and the stalker both. It seemed perfectly logical.

The Stalker's Tale

———◆———

A long session on the phone to the Professor – Donald, my very dear friend and mentor in the north. As well as being the world expert on such diverse subjects as military and naval history, the war and the earlier works of the Goons, he reads prolifically, and loves books on travel as much as those on sport. He taught me everything I know about stalking, and a very great deal more besides, including the finer points of darts which we'd play for hours in the cellar after a good day on the hill. I'd rung him early in the evening. 'Am I interrupting anything Prof.?' 'Well by God, if it's no' yerself – och no, as a matter o' farct, I wuz just givin' a gin and tonic hell, if you must know' and off we went for an hour or so's blather: information, gossip – most of it scurrilous – tales and stories, much laughter... Nothing changes: it's exactly how we've always spent most of our time together, both on the hill and off.

He was telling me about the funeral he'd been to 'this last back end', after his old stalker chum Bob Bisset had died up in Glen Lyon. (Bisset, with whom Donald had worked many years back, had taken me out stalking a couple of times when I'd stayed up in Glen Lyon; a famous character, he collected clocks and made boots and fiddles, and had a legendary knowledge of the verse of Rabbie Burns which he would declaim vociferously to the hills after you'd shot a stag.) He'd been given a particularly fine send-off, it appears, with a long session in the front room after. 'An' the auld bugger'd have really enjoyed it – fine great drams yez could smack yer lips over, and some of the boys in their stalking suits an' all.' It sounded grand.

I reminded him of the time we had discussed our own funerals and what we each wanted. Mindful of that nice line added, by a very respected author and stalking shot, to the Celtic blessing ('and may the garron carry you away'), I'd had a notion of having my ashes taken up on the pony and scattered at the top of a certain hill on the estate overlooking the sea, so long as Donald would do it; but then we reckoned the wind was always particularly hairy up there and it could be a bit grisly. He'd then said that, as far as he was concerned, all he wanted was a great big stone placed as a cairn, near the bridge at the far end of the stalking road where the deer come down to feed at night. 'And if I'm still around to see to it Prof., what do you want carved on the stone? How's about "The Finest Stalker in Argyll"?' 'Wail now...aye... But, hang on a minutey: "The Finest Stalker in Scotland" would look a darn'd sight baitter, ah'm thinkin'...'

We gossiped on about stalking generally, before he started to tell me the latest story he'd just heard. Apparently one of the estates on the west coast had an exceptionally good stag on the ground that they'd been watching for several years, and which they reckoned was now about 15 or 16. He had a lovely huge big wild head on him, on which the tops were just beginning to go back, so this season was clearly the right time to take him. The stalking guest that week was an old friend of the estate, a good shot who'd taken more than his fair share of rubbish off the hill over the past years, so it had generally been agreed by Management that he should be given the honour of being allowed to take this really fine beast.

The day dawned fine, the guest and Dougie the head stalker took to the hills and, after a couple of hours' climbing, by late morning had reached a high sort of ledge along the far end of the ground. Generally considered a good spying point, there's a gentle slope that runs up from it to the base of more hills on either side, with a long steep gully and corries in between; and through these gullies, beyond and up at the top, is another flattish piece of ground with a big black loch in the bowl of it, right on the march. The two men lay on a large rock, comfortable and taking a rest after their hard climb up, chatting together companionably (as you do) and spying the ground above them. A few groups of beasts around, and some hinds on the topmost ridge, and solitary stags dotted about the knolls, but no sign of Himself as yet.

A nice bit of breeze to keep the flies away, and they waited happily to see if anything else appeared. Then suddenly, he was there.

His long wide antlers like a great bow wave, the big old stag was climbing slowly but steadily away from them, up and along the side of one of the hills, making for the top ground where the loch was. And the march. Only one thing for it – a heart-busting headlong climb up to the top to cut him off.

Now Dougie, professional and fit, could climb like he was the reincarnation of Reinhold Messner. But the guest – long in years, out of condition and (like most guests) probably too much claret the previous night – was not in such good shape. He made extremely heavy weather of what was, admittedly, very hard-going at speed, and was gasping and wheezing by the time they finally scrambled over the top. The stag was still there, some 180 yards off; but he had obviously sensed them, or heard them, or caught their wind through the gully perhaps, as he was standing three-quarters away and looking back. 'If ye think ye can manage it sir' Dougie whispered urgently, 'a deep neck shot would do it… but ca' canny now – and ye'll have to hurry as he's seen us.'

Dougie said later that he would regret that remark for a long while. Still struggling to catch his breath and in an awkward lie, the guest took a hurried shot. It hit too far back; the beast took off and, to Dougie's astonishment, immediately made for the black loch where it stumbled in and began to swim. 'He wuz going like the clappers, out to the deep bit in the middle. So I told the man to stay where he wuz an' I grabbed the rifle an' ran towards the water, yellin' blue murder so the beast'ud turn off to the far shore, as I knew I could get him easy once he come out the water… He was swimmin' like the devil an' thrashin' away, an' then, bugger me – one minute he wuz there, the next minute he'd gone. Ninety yards out, and the damned thing'd just sunk. Like a ruddy stone …I couldna believe ma eyes… No' a flamin' sign o' him… And there's me left standin' there, cursin' and blindin' an' swearin' like an eedgit at a heap o' bloody bubbles…'

As Dougie stood there venting his fury, the guest came lumbering up. 'I thought he wuz goin' to cry. I felt quite sorry for the puir mannie in farct: it was no' a good shot mind ye, but it wasna his fault the bugger sunk… An' then I thought, *Cheeses*, he's gone an' shot the finest-ever beast offa ma ground, an' I'm goin' to look

a bloody fule in the larder tonight when the laird comes in: 'Yes sur we got the big stag, an' no sur, I'm afraid he's no hangin' up right now as he's still in the middle o' the effin loch'... That'll be me an' me P45 on the road afore dawn, likely. Hell no. So I reckoned we'd best go down the hill again, go back to the lodge an' call up the diver-laddie, he'd sort it out fer us fine.'

So they did that. The diver (actually the under-keeper on one of the neighbouring estates, whose hobby was deep-sea diving off the coast) was summoned, and climbed the hill to the loch early that afternoon with his tanks and his ropes and his flippers and his mask together with Dougie, who by this time had both a large hack-saw and a small rubber dinghy on his back. The two of them set forth into the loch, Dougie bobbing about in the rubber dinghy shouting final instructions to the lad swimming beside him: '... an' if it won't budge, jus' hack the bloody heid off, right?'

Which is exactly what happened. The delicate matter of salvage was resolved over a couple of bottles of malt much later that night.

The High Tops

'I had just returned from India' wrote the Marchioness of Breadalbane in *The High Tops of Blackmount*, 'and the men were never tired of listening to stories of sport in the jungle, and of the manner of such things in the Far East; but it always ended with the same paean that, after all, there is no country like Scotland, and no sport like stalking.'

She obviously agreed with them. In her long tweed skirts and her hat shaped like a soda-bread loaf she scoured the hills with Grant, her favourite stalker, and then wrote gloriously purple prose about her adventures on the equally 'almost purple rim' of her beloved high tops. She was probably the only lady who regularly took a rifle to the hills in the late nineteenth century.

There is a reference in Lord Malmesbury's memoirs to Lady Seymour, stalking in 1845 at Achnacarry; but stalking really was a man's sport then – the ladies would watch from a distance, possibly from the comfort of a barouche or having walked a little way, like Queen Victoria who left it to Albert to rise 'at five o'clock to go out deerstalking' and then 'walked out with the Duchess of Norfolk'. Perhaps, like the inn at Dalwhinnie that incurred her displeasure for 'no pudding, and no FUN', stalking was not much 'fun' for the onlookers. In August 1591 Queen Elizabeth I, together with the Countess of Kildare, had shot deer; but that was in a Sussex paddock and from under 'a delicate bowre' (sic) and with musicians and a cross-bow – an altogether less strenuous affair.

Even nowadays ladies are regarded, if not exactly an anomaly, at least as still just rather unusual on the hill. Stalkers blanch when you turn up for the regulation shots at the iron target or at a piece of boot-blacked paper. I once went to stalk at another

estate bearing, like an emissary, my credentials, a letter from one head-keeper to the other. This was read slowly and silently in front of me by a man whose furrowed brow and thunderous mien gave me no reason to suppose that I could look forward to anything other than a stout day's tramp about the hills. However at the end of the perusal his expression lightened, the atmosphere changed, and we set off for what turned out to be a wonderful and successful and very entertaining day. 'Whatever did you write Donald?' I enquired some time later, back home again. 'Wailll... it was, as you might say, a covering note, in case he wasna used to havin a wumman out wi' him. I just told the mannie that takin' yerself out would be nae mair bother to him than if he just shot the beast himself.' It was the greatest compliment I could have been given.

Modern stalking, as has often been observed, has not changed radically since the earliest days. Even though you may now start off in a Land Rover or a van, and the beasts may be collected off the hill by means of an ATV or a quad bike instead of the traditional pony, yet what Fraser Darling called 'the field-craft and physical stamina to come within 100 yards of a vigilant quarry in open country' remains (despite the 'modern' invention of a telescope sight on the rifle) the primary part and real motivation of a stalk. In *A Victorian Boyhood*, L.E.Jones wrote of 'the suspense, the alertness of observation, the pitting of wits, the triumph or the failure, which are the ingredients of delight'; and of 'the breathtaking beauty of the high tops... the solitariness and the silence' which together 'combine to exalt the spirit to the summit of happiness.' In truth, nothing has changed. And at the end of the day, there is still the long walk home, gossiping endlessly, as the hills turn pink in the dusk and the sun sinks like a canteloupe melon. It is the time of kelpies and the faery world, beloved of Scrope, when ghosts walk abroad.

But the ghosts of the hill do not always wait for dusk. Even Scrope's stalker Murdoch, a doughty man, got within shot of a hind on a hill called The Doune in broad daylight, only to see the beast transformed into a young woman. And I was told of a strange incident by the man to whom (according to him at any rate) it had happened – an old Islay keeper called Iain whose only acknowledgement of an after-life consisted in keeping a spare bottle of whisky 'to be put in the box with me when I'm buried, just in case like'.

One day in early August, he said, he set off on 'the wee ferry' over to Jura, (which lies about a mile to the northeast of Islay, across the stretch of water called The Sound) to take a turn about the hills there and have a look at the deer on the ground. He walked for a couple of hours into the heart of the island (habitation on Jura is mainly around the shoreline), then decided to rest awhile and have his lunch, sitting on a nice high rocky bit with his back to the hill from whence he could view the scenery below.

As he sat there quietly enjoying his piece, there was a rattle of stones from the shale above and a big old stag came leaping over him, right where he was resting, and went bounding off down the hill. Iain, thanking his lucky stars that he hadn't got trodden on, put up his binoculars to watch the stag and continued munching his piece. Moments later, there was another rattle of stones on the shale, and this time it was a deer-hound that came jumping over him, and followed off down the track the stag had taken. A few minutes passed, while Iain sat there, puzzled, trying to think of who it could be that had deer-hounds working on their bit of ground 'when, by God, another rattle of stones, an' the sound of someone panting real heavy, out o' breath, an' a small man come leaping down and followed away down the track after the dog an' the stag.'

There wouldn't have been anything particularly strange in all that really, except that, watching the little man running off down the hill, Iain noticed that he was wearing a strange type of leggings, all bound like thongs up to his knees, and carrying a bow, and a quiver-full of arrows. And he suddenly realised that, in the middle of a bright sunny day, 'an' with not a drop taken save some water from the burn', he had seen a hunting party of ghosts.

Good Dog

O ne of the more memorable lines to emanate from the Edinburgh Festival one year was made by an American comedian. Explaining his origins, he said that he came from Montana, a land 'so flat you could watch your dog running away for three days'.

I liked that. And it seemed somehow familiar – most of us have been there, haven't we? That moment of unutterable, desperate, impotent shame, when you're on a smart shoot, standing quietly waiting in line at the beginning of what is reputed to be the best drive of the day, and a rabbit skits past... And the normally highly-trained, biddable, perfectly-mannered hound suddenly takes a notion into what passes for his tiny skull and, as suddenly and single-mindedly as a crusader after the Holy Grail, takes off. No warning, just instant reflex action. And despite all your screaming and fury and whistling and admonitions and promises of instant demise upon his return, the dog's away – deaf and concentrating like fury, barking like a maniac, across the landscape towards the woods and, inevitably, in the direction of the drive and the beaters... Short of falling on your sword there and then, there's nothing you can do about this particular *dégringolade*, whilst your host, never the mildest of men and especially vitriolic on a shooting day, goes critical. And the rest of the line – guns, spectators on their shooting-sticks, pickers-up, everyone else's immaculately-behaved, silent (seated) dogs – watches, with the air reeking of *schadenfreude*, as huge flurries of birds take off in alarm and (of course) in the wrong direction...

I saw a sign in a Toulouse shop window once, which read: '*Chien fort mechant et peu nourri*' which seemed to encapsulate the vast difference between the canine-human relationships as practiced on the Continent and in this country. There, they keep dogs to do things like guard, worry, herd, retrieve, eat strangers etc. Here, we keep dogs who may do the same sort of things but (with the possible exception of Her Majesty's corgis, who are reputed to have the foulest tempers around) seem to do them with considerably more charm. For instance at the airport the other day I saw a sniffer-dog at work. There had been a programme on the television some time ago about how these dogs are trained: some are sleek, Mafioso-type Dobermans who look as of they should be wearing shades; some are furry Alsatian puppies, some are placid Labradors; all of them obviously love their handlers, and the element of 'play' is never far from the training programme and, indeed, is greatly encouraged. The one I saw in action was a spaniel, full of excitement and *joie de vivre*, ears flying, bustling with exuberance, breathless excitement and a desire to please. But then, that's spaniels all over.

My daughter's one arrived wearing a label from Father Christmas when she was four. A large tri-colour cocker who never really lost his puppy fluff, he had the sweetest nature and oodles of charm. He was also very amenable, not to say polite, and would sing whenever asked which was nice, especially at birthdays or Christmas. 'C'mon Benj, how's about Hark the Herald?' we'd cry and off he would go, rowling away, chin up and whiskers a-flutter. I sent him off to a trainer for six months when he was of age to learn some shooting etiquette; but he came back so cowed and miserable that we all felt it wasn't worth persisting, and it took a good six months before the wiggle and the busy tail returned. However he never lost a real terror of flexes or hoses: he must have been thrashed out of his mind by that man.

Understandably therefore, Benj promptly put any training he might have learned firmly out of his mind and, in the field, would merely sit on runners (his favourite task) until rescued. There was, however, one memorable occasion at home in Scotland when he managed to find, pick and bring back a woodcock, to the prolonged cheers of the whole line and, clearly, rather to his own surprise. My daughter then asked Donald whether he thought Benj was ok as a shooting dog, even though he didn't seem to know how to do it very well. 'Wail, pet' came Donald's thoughtful reply, 'I always say one thing about dogs. If yuz go' a dog, then it's the best bloody dog there is. Yuz just keep him hard by during the drives, an' he'll do fine.' They went round together after that, two small intense figures, one talking hard, and attached to each other on a string, which was brilliant as it saved everybody from having to look for them separately.

One of the best shooting dogs I ever saw belonged to a girl who was a regular picker-up at a friend's shoot. She had trained the dog, a huge yellow Labrador with a lovely square head, herself. She never shouted at it, or whistled, or indeed, during drives, spoke to it all. They communicated silently and by gesture alone. As they stood together behind you, the dog would watch you raise your gun and then would fixedly watch the bird down, marking it, sometimes turning and standing up on its hind legs to watch where it fell across a field, or if it was a runner. At the end of the drive, a small movement of the girl's hand and he was off. He also retrieved the birds in the exact order in which they had been shot.

As team-work, it was most impressive. Between drives she would make a great fuss of him and he would bounce round and smile a lot (I've always liked that bit in *Xenophon's Instructions to the Cavalry* where he advocates: 'Make much of your horses'); then the next drive would begin and there would be this big yellow dog, silently locking onto the birds like a missile, with an intensity that was quite remarkable. I had a theory he was deaf, and had learned to lip read, but apparently this wasn't so. The only upsetting moment came when you'd had a really rotten drive and had missed everything. At the end-of-drive horn the dog would stand up, yawn and stretch rather ostentatiously, then go over to a clump of grass or a bush and lift its leg, looking at you all the while. It was the most apt gesture of contempt.

Another memorable dog belonged to a friend of ours, a bishop, who regularly came to stay during the autumn for some stalking and the odd day out with a gun. It was late August and this particular day, Donald had decided, was just right for the bishop to try for his first Macnab – the brace of grouse, the stag and the salmon. Usually you start with the salmon as it's more difficult and unpredictable but today, having checked the forecast, they were first going up the hill for the stag and the grouse.

Later that afternoon, an eleven-pointer and a brace of grouse

in the back, the party – together with the bishop's dog who never left his side and even always went stalking with him – arrived down at the river where I was waiting for them with a little refreshment. Donald and I and the dog then moved back to sit together above the river and watch the bishop try for the final part. The dog, a black Labrador called Amin (the bishop always named his Labradors after prominent African personalities), was very quiet, never stirring but watching his master's every move.

The three of us sat there for about two hours. It had to be said that, although as a fisher of men he excelled, the bishop's prowess on the river bank left a great deal to be desired. As far as fishing went, he was a real disaster. Finally, the dog had obviously had enough of this ineptitude. He rose to his feet, walked slowly down the bank to stand by his master and, looking up, wagged his tail and began to whimper. The bishop looked down at him, sighed, and slowly reeled in his line. 'O all RIGHT' he said, rather petulantly, to the dog. 'Let's see if YOU can do any better then.' The dog jumped into the water, disappeared under the surface, and emerged after about 15 seconds bearing a nice flapping salmon.

Donald's entry in the game book that evening – 'A fine Macnab, achieved by The Bishop and Labrador Amin' – looked rather splendid.

Male Bonding

There's the occasional odd moment when I think what fun it must be to be a man. No, not a closet trans-sexual, I wouldn't not be a woman for anything; but it's just that sometimes all that men-only stuff looks rather fun and enviable: regimental ceremonials, Formula One or All Souls, or the Jockey Club or stag nights or team photos in the gents' loo or the front stair-case at The Garrick... Of course it's not as if men didn't allow any women at all to be part of these scenarios ('Lord no, I mean to say, we have to employ *cleaners* for heaven's sake...') but I guess, for the purist, only White's and the papacy are the remaining unsullied bastions. It's just that with the envy comes the rather shaming realisation that, when men *really* want to enjoy themselves, they'd rather do so with other men.

Absolutely right of course. Male bonding is a deep and beautiful thing, friendship pure and between two souls, and totally wrecked by the presence of females. Women inhibit. All very well in their right place of course and all that, but you can't really, I mean REALLY, get to grips with proper serious *manly* things when they're hanging around wittering. Things like mediaeval philosophy, or political science, or the struggle for power, or global finance, or drink. That's it, isn't it? Therein lies the real rub; whether it's the 'pass-the-port-dear-boy' or the 'arlaf-annuvah-fanks' variety, male bonding is ultimately about drinking together. This isn't just a modern phenomenon either. Take early cave-life, or woad-covered forest dwellers; or think of Angles and Saxons, those fine specimens of upstanding manhood, wearing

last year's broth and with B.O. you could carve and body-hair like hearth rugs, setting off for a spot of rapen'pillage of an afternoon: they must have looked forward to the men-only sessions of mead-induced blotto later, on the hey-ho-the-rushes-o... *Plus ça change...*

I was explaining this profound theory to Donald one evening as the two of us sat in the gun room enjoying a quiet dram after a particularly good day and putting the rifle to bed, and he started to laugh. 'Wail now... ah mind the time...' he began (it never took long to get him going) and launched into an account of the day when he and Duncan (the erstwhile head-keeper) had been doing one of the winter shoots. Duncan, as was his wont, had been somewhat over-indulgent with the 'refraishments' over lunch which, together with some beers he'd discovered earlier and which clearly needed dealing with then and there, had rendered him steadily less and less coherent as the afternoon wore on.

The guns were slowly moving into the long back wood for the last drive. It was one of those nice easy shooting parties where everyone was having fun, the sport had been good and the weather fine and now they were all taking their time, loth to hurry the end of a great day. There was no rush anyway as the beaters still had to take in a couple of spinneys and some kale up at the top end before the drive would start, while Duncan and Donald were dealing with the far side of the wood, up by the stone wall and out in the fields beyond, where a couple of runners had been seen to come down during the previous drive. Donald was working his dog close inside the wall, and could hear Duncan working his out in the fields, whistling (a bit uncertainly) now and again, and doing lots of 'goodog' and 'clever girrul' and 'welldone lass, bring it here'. He decided to cross over the wall and give them a hand as Duncan wasn't really in the best of shape, and clearly there was more than he'd thought to pick in the field.

He heaved his spaniel across the wall and climbed over. There was no sign of Duncan out in the field but he could still hear him burbling away to the dog; so he advanced out some twenty yards or so and then looked back to see where they'd got to. And there, propped up against the wall, his yellow Labrador bitch with one eye open and her head on his knee, sat Duncan – a half-bottle of whisky in one hand, the old Players No.6 in the other – taking his ease in the warm fading sunlight. And every so often, punctuating his conversation with the whisky bottle with further earnest-sounding exhortations to the recumbent dog beside him: 'clever girrul, whereisit... good lass... goodog...' and the odd hiccup.

Donald couldn't believe his eyes. 'Ah thought to maself Christ, he's had a stroke... An' the auld rogue, he just turned and looked at me an' winked. "C'mon, sit down an' take a dram" sez he. "There's plenty time." An' there was, too. So ah did, and by God it was good. So we finished the bottle between us an' ah burried it up under the wall an' it'll be there still, ah'll be bound. Then ah left him asleep against the wall and we did the last drive jus' fine and dandy, an' ah come back fer him arter, an' carried him to ma' car and drove him home, an' not a soul was the wiser. The auld devil.'

'An' d'ye know,' added Donald, replenishing his glass as an afterthought, 'the bugger once caught me tryin' to poach his wife an' he went fer me; but arter that, we never had a cross word between us. A good man, so he wuz.'

Weight of Numbers

S o, someone finally solved Fermat's Last Theorem – that ele-
gantly-named and hitherto Greatest Unsolved Puzzle in
mathematics. One Mr. Wiles, clever fellow, claimed the
spoonful of jam, the Wolf Prize for Mathematics and, frankly, I'm
envious. Numbers, congruent or otherwise, don't sing to me and
there are times I wish they did if only not to appear such a complete dolt. 'Look' they say kindly, 'it's so SIMPLE ...' and of course
it is – even I can see that – but I just can't get to grips with it.

'Yes, well... gotta watch the pressures haven't you? I mean it's
an MV of twosixty after all and you can't muck around with that.'
Erm... 'Especially with a ten-inch twist.' Oh definitely. And we're
not in Casualty here either: it's a perfectly straightforward discussion concerning the alternative methods of hand-loading rifle
ammunition. Listen to a bunch of CPSA fanatics in their club-
house and it's the same thing. 'Well now, you should try a multi-
choke grade five with a thirty-inch spout and an s/s pull, that's

more the job. And faster squibs – say eleven-fifty p.s. – makes all the difference.' This sort of thing just makes my eyes water.

In the *old* old days, a gentleman shot didn't concern himself with such things. If he shot Match Rifle, that leisurely and civilised past-time over the long ranges at Bisley, he would blow the spiders out of the barrel once a year before the Imperial Meeting (a gentleman never went down to practice or anything as swotty as that, of course), despatch a minion for a supply of army-issue .303 from the armoury, then simply lie down and, in the words of a legendary old Chairman of the NRA, 'just *make* the bugger shoot'. No computing, no ballistics other than the universally accepted rise between ranges, and no handloads then of course, just look at the wind flags and get on with it. As for things with feathers on, his factor would order forty thousand cartridges at the beginning of each season, delivered on pallets at the Tremmens Entrance, and the gentleman could then take out one of his grandfather's old pairs of Grants or Woodwards and enjoy a decent day at the Englishmen or on the grouse moor. 'An ounce of Number 7' was probably the only technically-orientated phrase to cross his lips. Any other details were noted down by some clerk in the huge mouse-nibbled leather-bound ledger, in longhand, using a quill pen. Great days for the shooting man.

Nowadays, you still really don't have to know much more than how to add two or three to stand in a line of guns. But it's worth listening to your host – the worst ones are usually highly-paid financiers – to learn how to make a proper meal out of the calculus. 'Now I know we're *really* moving two-up-three-down, but on the next drive Archie has to be walking gun down the middle so he can pick up his car at the other end so everyone moves one place *less* than normal which means – you with us George? – that if you were 5 on the last drive you *should* be 8 this drive but you'll actually be on 7, no hang on, that's wrong, odd numbers go down don't they so you'd *really* be 2, no, 3, that's it, gottit now – clear everyone?' And all the guns – who've had a jolly good lunch and far too much liquid refreshment in the warm fug of the pub, and who have already been fully taxed

mathematically trying to work out the bar orders, and actually couldn't give a fig one way or the other – stand about flushed and swivel-eyed silently praying that they won't have to put their gun up to anything at all for the remainder of the afternoon, or indeed meet any of the boys in blue on the way home.

Numbers, in the context of the total bag, are really immaterial (unless you are going for a record which anyhow isn't *really* the done thing in most circles nowadays). Small mixed bags are the most fun of all.

We were out rough-shooting one beautiful November day in Scotland with Donald; it was clear and bright and, not content with just walking up hedgerows, we were into the more serious commando stuff: poaching the odd pheasant across the river, crawling over fields to ambush geese and creeping round hillocks for a rabbit. Variety was the name of the game and we'd got a highly satisfactory small, very mixed, bag which included a couple of woodcock plus a hoodie and a stray cat. The dark was beginning to draw in so we'd decided to call it a day when Donald decided on one last Cunning Plan, a manoeuvre across an open bit of moorland and down to the small burn where the cattle got fed, before getting back home and shooting hats in the headlights down the back drive.

The moorland bit was the most productive: a snipe and two hares and, surprisingly, a blackcock out of a small fir plantation towards the burn. Once by the water – heavy whinn bushes on either side and a nice burbly bit where it ran shallow over stones – Donald stopped. 'We'll just go slowly down the side a hundred yards or so' he whispered. 'Go quietly now, an' keep as low as ye can.' We crouched into that particularly awkward half-open-penknife stance reminiscent of Groucho Marx and, guns ported, stumbled along. Someone slipped in a cowpat and cursed. Donald's dog, after being growled to heel, obviously felt that this was all seriously frustrating and was making those o-for-heavens-sake-let-me-*past* lunges ... It was very quiet, and you could hear the grouse going to bed up the hill. A roe doe barked, somewhere near. Suddenly Donald froze in front of us. 'DUCK' he hissed, urgently.

Finely-honed deer-stalkers all, instantly obedient to the least command, we dropped unquestioningly and silently to the ground, our faces tucked low into thistles, bog and bramble. At the same moment there was a great flurry in the water just in front of us and half a dozen fine mallard took off as one into the darkness, shouting derision.

Donald sat down on the bank and laughed and laughed until

he began to choke and had to be hit on the back. But he did say later that, although as wildfowlers we left a lot to be desired, we were, 'daifinitely', the most biddable stalking party he'd ever been out with.

In the Best of Spirits

———◆———

I was at my peg waiting for the second drive to begin, surreptitiously feeling out (the beaters had got quite a bit of ground to bring in, so there was lots of time) the contents of the shooting jacket pocket, making sure I'd got a clean handkerchief and the lip-gloss, when all at once I knew it had happened. It was as nasty as discovering that the cat's thrown up in one of your boots. Amongst all the usual detritus I always carry around in my shooting jacket (chewing-gum, lighter, knife, plasters, aspirins, arnica, etc. – well, you never know) there was a thick, sticky, tacky, colloid, glutinous and viscous mess... And after a second I realised exactly what it had to be – the cork in the top bit of my hip-flask had gone, and so had the whisky.

On a tidy, rather formal shoot, at this sort of moment you can't do the only really sensible thing, namely unload your gun, rip the jacket off, hold the thing upside down and let the miasmic gunge just drip out. All you can do is braille your way through the sodden bits and pieces without yelping *uhhh-yukkkk* or making a scene, either of which would be considered Bad Form.

I couldn't think why I had the flask anyway, but then remembered that it must have been a left-over from the week before when I'd been stalking, and when I'd patently failed to clear out the pockets afterwards. I never drink whisky myself, but always feel that a hip-flask might come in handy Just In Case, either out on the hill (adder bite perhaps?) or if someone needed life-saving when punt-gunning, or shooting geese in mid-winter.

One winter in Scotland, we'd been asked by the neighbours to join them flighting geese – a masochistic past-time involving long hours at dawn or dusk waiting in the worst possible weather with perhaps, if you were lucky, the odd chance of a shot. That particular morning, everything was ideal: 5am, pitch dark and perfectly filthy, with winds of 'gale-to-storm force 10 increasing' and horizontal rain, the sort of conditions you read about in lifeboat citations. The ground was like quagmire as the neighbour's keeper Willy and I, bent double against the elements, trudged the half-mile or so from the road across fields and ditches to where I was going to be placed for the duration. There were rabbit-holes everywhere, we'd had to negotiate three barbed-wire fences which I hadn't managed too well in the dark, and I was already regretting my warm bed.

'Now you sit in there mum' Willy shouted encouragingly against the gale, indicating a small drain under a fence, hemmed in by gorse bushes. 'Mind where the cows... ach well, it's no' easy seen... The birds'll start comin' over in about an hour... whaz-zatye sayin'?... No, ye're nowhere near the others, they're all away in the fields a mile or so yonder, up by the sea wall; but you just stay put, right? An' don't be stirrin' out the ditch now. I'll come back later with the dog... no idea, but you jus' sit tight in there and either meself or the boy'll come for you when we're all done. That's you right then?' and holding on to his cap, he disappeared into the stormy darkness.

There's not a lot to be said for crouching in a ditch, in the pitch black, in a Force 10, in some northern fastness of the British Isles, in the middle of December. Even with full waders (which anyway I'd snagged on one of the barbed-wire fences) and water-proofs, and skiing socks and every thermal known to modern science, you freeze. I froze. The drain was deep and full of what seemed to be silage effluent, some of which had unerringly found the torn bits of the waders and had travelled down into one boot. There was no way of getting even marginally comfortable, thanks to the attentions of the wind-maddened gorse bushes but – hey – that's goose-flighting for you. Juddering with cold, I waited for the dawn.

Finally it came and, with it, the barnacle geese. High, in their thousands, calling and talking their way in from the sea against a metal-grey sky. Nothing came remotely within range, but in the distance I could hear the odd shots... maybe they were having some luck away over there. A sliver of sky lightened, just for show, then the clouds came again and patched it up. The wind howled like a mad thing. I crouched miserably in my ditch, numb to the bone.

The hours ticked by. Thank heavens I'd got my watch. By eight o'clock I was so cold I couldn't move. The wind was perish-ing, the rain hadn't let up except once, briefly, when it hailed.

Skeins of geese moved round very high, heavy clouds came and went, but no goose came over my field. Just as well: despite the gloves, my hands seemed to have frozen solid and I couldn't have even got the gun up, let alone the safety catch off.

Half past nine came and went. The sound of shots seemed to have stopped a while ago, but Willy'd told me to stay put... By now I'd unloaded the gun and was hunched up in a ball and heard myself moaning into the gale; if he or his boy didn't come soon they'd find me rooted there under the gorse bushes, turned to stone, ice-bound... bet the Ice Man of the Alps was out goose-flighting, that fateful day... hell, even Shackleton hadn't had to suffer like this – and at least he'd been able to move around hadn't he? Have to keep alert somehow... good idea, try talking out loud, dear God, this is just awful... And then I remembered the hip-flask. I also remembered I didn't drink, but this was an emergency. Had I put it in the jacket? Yes. *Miraculo*. O mercy, thank you, praise be to all the saints...

I managed to retrieve the flask from an inside pocket with some difficulty. Getting the top off was a problem as I was shaking and fumbling like an idiot from the cold. I then managed to drop the screw-on top, which vanished straight down into the drain. Oh well, too bad... The flask was filled to the brim and I hate the smell but come on girl, just do it, slurp some down... *Wow*. Gosh. That was good... Didn't realise whisky was like this, you could feel it melting its way down... another gulp perhaps, just to make sure the first one wasn't lonely... Not too bad really, maybe just another small slug...

Actually, come to think of it, since the top had vanished, no way of putting the thing back in a pocket anyway, so probably most intelligent thing was to swig the lot. Not too fast of course; and they'd come soon please God and find me and meanwhile I'd just get this inside me, purely medicinal of course, helps stave off hyperthermals, no, hypoth... whatever... can't be long now...

Some considerable time later I was hallucinating: there was this warm breath, and a warm muzzle on my face... 'Are ye there mum?' Willy, plus dog, loomed up; 'are ye still there?' I raised my head, waved in what I hoped was a nonchalant manner, tried to stagger to my feet and fell over, beaming happily. 'Ach fer God's sake wifey, are ye all right?'

It transpired, so they told me later, that the others had all been collected by Willy's boy and then had driven home. *At half past nine*. Baths, then Black Velvet and a huge breakfast: several geese had been shot, everyone in tremendous form and – *around eleven* mind you – in the middle of the banter and the black pudding and the coffee and the kedgeree, some bright spark FINALLY notices I'm not there… Panic ensued, someone went to ring Willy's house, he'd understood the boy had collected everyone and so had gone off with the dog to look for a bird that had come down by the forestry so he'd only just come in himself…

I don't remember how we got to Willy's car, the drive back, anything. But apparently I'm really charming when smashed. It was past midday when we got home. Someone put me to bed, and I slept the sleep of the righteous until the following day.

Finders Keepers

Were I to be asked to name some of the nicest people I'd ever met, there would be a lot of stalkers and keepers at the top of the list. Not all of course: as in every walk of life – journalism, banking, garbage collection, politics, the church, you name it – there will always be the odd souls with whom you just don't, for some inexplicable reason, click… But these, happily, are few and far between anyway and, as with certain folk who once were in your address book and now have been deleted – the mildest form of megalomania, but so satisfying – you can cross them off your Christmas card list. Most keepers and stalkers I have met are people I'd actually like to have with me at all times. Especially on a desert island.

A hard life, being a keeper. I'm not talking about the daily grind, the sheer slog, the 24-hour-a-day, 365-day-a-year commitment, the unending workload, the physical demands, the hassles – and let's not forget the occasional dangers either… No; it's the fact that all this has to be combined with devotion, charm, imagination, good-humour and wit, as well as the patience of doves and the diplomacy of snakes. Plus the fact that the temptation to smash a lot of faces must be very trying to have to endure on a daily basis, and should be emphasised in the job spec. Quite like married life, come to think of it.

Have you noticed how good every head-keeper is at being totally non-committal? I'm sure it's genetic, part of the inherited knowledge. So, to his boss's regular road-to-Damascus lightning-strikes of genius ('Hey, why not put a couple more duck-ponds in there? ' or 'I really feel there aren't enough traps around' or 'but, that's easy, surely – just double the amount of dung on the snipe-bogs'); or to the thousand and one brilliant ideas/hints/knowhatimeanmate's he has to endure from others who, like Toad, think they know everything there is to be knowed about The Countryside, the keeper just nods, says 'Uh huh' and goes away to kick things, quietly and alone.

Apart from dealing with the boss, and the team, and the farmers and the beaters and the neighbours and the poachers and the antis and the vermin, think of having to deal with shooting guests – half of them morons who couldn't hit a barn if they were inside it. 'Ah yes' you have to say kindly afterwards, 'but they were on the curl sir – very tricky indeed, but you didn't half do well at the second drive didn't you'; and also make encouraging noises to small boys *and* see the line's straight *and* not mutter obscenities about the guns or their dogs or their ineptitude *and* speak politely to the ladies *and* keep your temper at all times especially with old Tom who's drunk again and forgotten the beaters' beers and the boss's wife's bloody house-cat that's screwed up the duck drive as usual... Organising a shooting day must be hell - like *Gotterdammerung* without the jokes.

Of course there are compensations and, as the senior man, impressive in this season's new suit, you might as well make the most of it. 'A quiet word in your ear, sir' must be about the most chilling words for a gun to hear from the head-keeper at the end of a drive. The question (actually of course it's not a question, it's a statement) that I always dread is 'Nothing to pick here madam?' combined with a very obvious glance at the pile of empty cartridges by the peg. Scottish head-keepers seem to have some of the best lines: like the old classic 'Dukes an' urruls wi' me, the rest o' the guns with the bee'ers'; or, said to a man purple in the face from screaming and whistling, in vain, across the moorland wastes: 'Aye, I seen a dog like that once. Didn't think much o'it.' Pause. 'Sho' it, as a matter o' farct'. And, by a river bank – straight-faced to a small child who'd just caught its first tiddler on a worm and was demonstrating to an audience its new-found casting skills: 'Hah – I've met buggers like you afore – one fish and yer a bloody expairt'.

As a head stalker of course, you are, to an even greater extent, lord of all you survey, so the opportunities are legion. A friend, noted for his regular prowling of corridors, was chastised for having missed a beast with the growl: 'If ye'd only leave the hinds at night ye'd surely have more success with the stags during the day. Sur'. Donald never minced his words but nevertheless was unfailingly polite to guests. The rest of us just came in for general verbal abuse on the lines of 'Och hell wumman, I'm no' takin' out annywan dressed like some bloody bedoueeen' – the greeting one

perishing snowy December morning as, wrapped up in every available rug, coat, scarf and muffler, I climbed into his car before setting off for the hill after the hinds.

We had both taken out rifles that day and, later in the afternoon – it really was foul and the weather was worsening fast into snow and freezing fog – after a careful and numbingly lengthy spy Donald decided that, in order to make the most of this final opportunity to get the half-dozen beasts needed, we should both shoot at the same time. So, in the teeth of arctic conditions and with suitable deliberation, we emptied our magazines in unison at our carefully-selected targets in the large herd of hinds huddled away in the white-out. It sounded like Pirbright. 'How many?' he asked, after we'd sat up and were blowing on frozen fingers and the ear-ringing had stopped. 'Oh God, dunno – can't talk – too cold – scope fogged up – three I think…You?' 'A puckle – family shots as ye might say.' The hillside was now eerily still and silent. We walked round and round the ghostly peat-hags for half an hour looking for bodies. All we found was one miserable knobber, dead with five shots in the head; and one very large boulder, heavily bullet-scarred.

Rather like the Eban tribe described by Desmond O'Hanlon, Donald – when he thought something was really funny – would sit down to laugh. He sat down.

Girl-Power

———◆———

Women are revolting. No no, I'm not denigrating any of my sex – what, *moi*? Heavens no. I'm merely saying that there seem to have been rustlings in the undergrowth of late, with certain women in revolt at perceived injustices from their male counterparts in the shooting field, writing accusatory letters to the press about 'discrimination amongst pickers-up' etc. etc. And signed 'Via e-mail' to boot... Should have been signed 'Via Dolorosa' really: the road to the shooting field is, especially for a woman, long and hard to tread.

I know nothing about being a picker-up on a shoot. However, I have met lots of ladies who are and who do their job brilliantly. Like Joan for instance: she is discreet and charming, her dogs are impeccable, her ready smile, under that smashing tweed hat, is a welcome ray of sunshine, especially when you've been shooting really badly, and she is, like all the other lady pickers-up I've ever encountered, a sweet and hardworking enthusiast who is univer-sally respected and loved, both by the other beaters and keepers and by all the members and guests of the shoots on which she works. If she were ever 'discriminated against', I would imagine it could only be on the grounds that she looks, I have to say – and they would undoubtedly agree – decidedly prettier than her male colleagues.

I don't remember the reasons the letter-writer gave for think-ing that, as a woman, she had been discriminated against as a picker-up. I can only state, again, the blinding truism that, in every known sphere of human society, you can get on better with some people than with others. However 'different' you are to the rest – which is after all the basis of discrimination – whether by sex, colour, race, creed or ability, you can still try overcoming any difficulty by the deployment of a combination of genes, pheronomes, auras, attitude, respect, humour and other mystic vibrations, some of which you can do nothing about and others which you have to work at. If someone takes an instant dislike to me, it's not necessarily discrimination, it's just that he or she patently doesn't like me. Reason? Don't know – could be anything at all; but I always reckon it's probably my fault so I'd just better mind my manners and my attitude the next time I meet them.

Men, it is true and we all know it, don't much like it if women are better than they are, at almost anything really except darning. And, understandably, everyone heartily dislikes anyone who whinges, or criticises, or who sets themselves up to be something they're not. However if men actually *discriminate* against us on any other grounds, it's probably merely because they imagine their masculinity is being threatened. This is of course where the really cunning woman – a Catherine the Great, say – does all that she can to dispel these feelings (however justified they may be), if only on the perfectly obvious grounds that life will be a good deal easier for her if she does. It's not exactly divulging the secret of Fatima to say that any woman's best weapons are her modesty, her generosity, her enthusiasm and her charm. 'Goodness-you-are-clever' is a phrase you will hear ringing throughout the breadth of the land, in offices, kitchens or work-places, in rocket labs and amongst brain surgeons, and indeed in the shooting field, every day of the week; and almost always spoken by a woman to a man. I'm no expert on this, mind you, but I reckon men are – or should be – a doddle if one can only master one's temper and not yell invectives or even suggest that they might usefully go and get knotted, but just smile sweetly and heap praise on them whenever possible. Rather like dealing with puppies.

Mind you, even some females in the shooting fraternity can be terrifying specimens. I once met a woman at the French Game Fair who, within the first five minutes of conversation, announced that she had already shot 117 different game species, including the Big Five, and was looking round so hungrily that everyone backed off fast. She looked wonderful too, which made it all the more galling – great figure, beautifully dressed, loads of tusks and elephant-tails and lion's claws hanging off gold chains, and with a retinue of admiring acolytes... I felt inferior and jealous. I later muttered things like Wow and Golly, but all the Englishmen around were noisily and gratifyingly dismissive: 'Heavens to betsy, what a frightful creature, and wearing that ghastly game rack thing round her neck – ridiculous. And zero charm, eh?...' 'Wouldn't have her out with me I can tell you. Can you just imagine her in a snipe bog, or walking up woodcock for goodness' sake – you'd be taking your life in your hands ...' 'Don't be so silly – what do you mean, she's got style... You silly woman: remember what Fats Waller said of swing? Lady, if ya gotta ask, you ain't got it. Give me a steady well-trained English lady gun on a shoot any day...' I could have kissed them.

Out of Line

———◆———

'Come on, nothing like a drop of something to make you shoot really well' cried our genial host, sploshing out the sloe gin in the yard where the pre-shoot meet was being held. 'Relaxes the nerves, you know, loosens up the swing and all that – there you go, hair of the dog...'

Nowadays I don't drink much except fizzy water most of the time – and wine; but then, three glasses of claret at dinner and that's me, trashed. (Not enough practice, that's what. Of course the remedy is perfectly easy, men do it all the time: get in training and drink a lot, every day, so the system gets used to it...) But knowing this, I don't ever drink the night before shooting, so that particular morning I was in cracking form. Unlike most of the rest of the party, it seemed. It was clearly going to be like one of those days immortalised by A.J.Stuart-Wortley in the *Fur, Feather and Fin* series of the 1890s; in *The Partridge* section, he writes fondly of enjoying 'the '74 champagne, the '40 port and the '20 brandy' but warns the reader that 'good living does not make for good shooting the next day'. He also describes, from what has to be first first-hand experience, 'that peculiar class of *"head"* which feels, after each shot, like the opening and closing of a heavy book, charged with electricity.'

Men don't ever have hangovers, have you noticed? It's 'a trifle under the weather', or 'not feeling Quite The Thing don't y'know' and they stand round in the yard looking ashen and trying to kick the dog and frowning at those little collar-stiffener things you get handed to pick your number which they can't read anyway as they're holding them upside down. Then it's everyone into the trailer and they're all sitting in there chewing mints and Rennies to conceal the Hoppes-like fumes and groaning when the wheels go over any bumps in the track... Halfway to the first drive, some plonker's realised he's left his gun on top of his car in the yard, and the rest of them are ready to kill him. And you wonder whether it's particularly wise to be standing in a line with these guys who'll be shooting probably badly but certainly over-aggres-

sively, like they're Master of the Universe ('charged with electricity' or not, you do that with a hangover just to prove you haven't got one), and whether it'll be what the pilots' manuals refer to as Marginal, and why the hell didn't you bring a flask of Fernet Branca which you could then administer surrreptitiously in the soup.

After lunch the earlier death-wish has been replaced (thanks to some quite decent red, followed by just a smidgin of port) with a nice, beamish, who-cares-anyway attitude. Any vestige of concentration has gone up the spout as all anyone wants to do now is sleep. (Actually this is perfectly normal on almost any shoot and simply means that, on the first drive after lunch, the ratio of cartridges fired to birds killed is increased usually by a factor of about eight – it's quite an interesting phenomenon.) So, on this particular day, here we all were after lunch in a deep gully at the bottom of cathedral-high plantations soaring up the hills all around. Luckily there had been a frost earlier in the week so the leaves had dropped, otherwise you could well have suffered the illusion of being in a natural *oubliette*. Listening to beaters working away, nothing much happening yet – and suddenly, there's this pigeon batting towards the line, miles up, oblivious.

Now I know that, unless you're walking with the beaters, you're not meant to fire at a pigeon before the drive's started properly (it's bad form, the birds break out, the keeper gets all ratty etc. etc.) so I was standing quietly, gun over the arm, just watching it. But someone chortled 'over' in a jokey sort of way and the old boy next to me, who'd been kipping gently on his feet like an ancient warhorse, awoke with a start and took instant action. Without a thought (he explained later) the old reflexes took charge: he swung up and let off both barrels almost as one (slippage, happens sometimes, hmm?) and down it came, dead as a doornail, into the trees behind us, to huge cheers from the rest of the line.

It was a brilliant shot and, to have pulled it off semi-comatose, with none of the little grey cells in gear, was remarkable. It was only when I when to retrieve it for him at the end of the drive that I saw the rings round its legs, glinting 'midst the leaves...

Pandemonium ensued. Worse than just the rings, it had its name, address *and telephone number* stamped inside both wings... Our host (who was quite cross about it actually – 'absolutely out of line Freddy, what the hell were you thinking of, heavens above... and anyway can't you tell the difference at your age' etc.) made all the right noises, took a note of the telephone number, ordered the wretched Freddy to pull himself together and do the responsible thing and phone the owner at the end of the day with some serious apologies, while the rest of us stood round and looked at this poor thing and felt like murderers.

I think it was the telephone number that really clinched it for me. It made it all that much more *personal*, somehow. I mean you could just imagine it, couldn't you, winging your way home on a lovely autumn afternoon, giving it your all and thinking about tea, don't worry mother I'm on my way, minding your own business – and suddenly this steaming great berk wakes up from his post-prandial ziz and radically changes your whole outlook ...

'Definitely need a good stiff one now' muttered the old warhorse. Who was it who said that 'we know little about the conscience, except that it is soluble in alcohol'?

Making an Impression

ccording to the advertising industry 'only 7% of commu-
nication is verbal; make the other 93% count'. Put like
that, it's quite scary; but it is after all the basis of those
infuriating nanny-like *dicta* we all suffered early on, of the 'first
impressions count' variety like 'always make sure your shoes
are clean, dear, as-you-never-know-who-you-might-meet'. My
dear friend Donald invariably worked on this premise: 'Why do
you *always* wash the van *before* we go out on the hill Professor?'
'Ach wail, ye naiver know, never hurts to be clean'n'tidy – ye jus'
might come across the Queen hersel' out the glen road, an' her
needin' a lift.'

First impressions are often surprisingly accurate; hence, if
you're a lonely heart, meeting under the station clock is a much
wiser option than the beguiling but faceless e-mail. Clothes are
usually a dead give-away – it's probably fair to say that a goodly
proportion of 'the other 93%' relies on turn-out for starters. My
mother, a corner-stone of illogical reasoning as was apparent
even to her own child, always told me never to speak to nuns on
trains, maintaining they were 'all rapists in disguise' – which did
absolutely nothing to improve those miserable rail journeys going
back to school.

Quite logically, each sex is best at assessing its own: men are
miles better at instantly summing up other men's appearance
than women. 'Hmm, something not quite right there, trousers too
tight' a man will say of another man, while you're still drooling
over the beauty of the profile. However they also come up with
things like 'but he was at school with me so he's quite sound'
which doesn't help, but does effectively stop any further argument. Likewise any woman can sum up another woman by her
clothes, at a single glance and totally instinctively, usually to the
fury of her male companion who is salivating, pretending he's
deaf and doesn't understand what the withering comment 'hook-
er heels' actually *means*. So it isn't exactly rocket science to work
out that, as far as the opposite sex is concerned, both men and

women base their first impressions on physical appearance. Surprise, surprise...

Now I know that in most chronically-retarded mysoginist circles, viz. gentlemen's clubs, masonic lodges etc., women are generally considered to be stultiloquent airheads, whose verbalisations are never confined to a mere 7%, and who can't remotely hack it in any situation where there isn't a mirror to hand. Although directed mainly at fair-haired girls, all of whom apparently have 'I'm a natural blonde, please speak slowly' tattooed on their foreheads, this generalisation is also expansively applied to anything female on a shoot, regardless of her root-colour. Men don't really go for women at all when shooting, as they're inclined to interfere with the job in hand and, even worse, to chat. Men hate chat – at breakfast, during drives, in the middle of the final half, at the *moment critique* in bed – it's wildly irritating. Anything that looks remotely glamorous is, moreover, regarded with deep suspicion in an arena where a female should in no way be remarkable and should anyway preferably have four legs. ('What do you call a blonde who can find things?' 'A retriever'.) Therefore, to make a good first impression on any man don't ever, if you're a woman, meet him to start off with on the shooting field where you will be perforce, and *simply by being a woman*, horribly disadvantaged.

Women on the other hand are always suckers for men who are fetchingly 'dressed up' for any occasion; hence Edwardian smoking jackets, or white tie with coloured facings, or lace cuffs and ancient kilts or wonderful waistcoats, all the hackneyed old regalia, make any woman an absolute push-over at any time. The shooting field has endless and obvious possibilities: I've always reckoned that anyone re-enacting the early attempts at 'Shooting Flying' (ie. clad in late-17th century kit of be-ribboned coat, full leather boots, long feathers adorning cavalier-style hat and probably yellow cross-gartering) would get my vote any day. Women are anyway impressed by gentlemen who shoot, as they are indulging in a historically-male sport for which they dress, on the whole, rather well. They wear clean, but not pressed, tweeds of a discreet pattern (in the States, men who wear 'loud' clothes, or brag unduly, are somewhat pithily referred to as being 'all hat, no cattle'); and for luncheon, if it's a relatively formal day, they will don a well-cut half-change jacket, with a silk handkerchief which is never folded but just tucked in anyhow into the breast pocket. They also wear leather shooting-boots and possibly amusing but invariably 'proper' shooting headgear.

Headgear, as far as making an impression on a woman in the shooting field, is a Good Thing, but the style is vital: a large fedora of any colour – other than emerald green – is acceptable but only if the wearer is under 40 and in Debrett's; a nice tweed shooting cap is perfect *so long as it doesn't look new* (run it over a couple of times, or drop it under the beaters' wagon before the first drive, if it's a recent purchase); and the grandfather's moth-eaten trilby is probably best of all. However, a pancake-style 'flat'at' is never a good idea – it's not even remotely becoming – or, even worse, a baseball cap, which is a real turn-off. Women likewise never go a bundle on men who actually choose to look as if they have the IQ of an ant, an impression easily given by anyone still wearing those gaily-coloured shooting stockings with words like 'Right' and 'Left' or 'Bang Bang' and 'Bugger' emblazoned around the turn-overs.

This is all fine and dandy but in fact, as we all know, men don't give a flying duck about what they wear, and women dress for other women who are the only ones who'll notice anyway; so first impressions based on sartorial criteria are actually, probably, totally unreliable – amongst the shooting fraternity at any rate. Modesty, politeness and charm, the obvious affection of one's friends and 'general tidiness and presentability' as it was called, speak volumes. As in so many things, Donald of course had it spot on.

Shooting Wives

It's lovely enough to be asked to shoot. Even more, to be asked to spend the night before; and sheer heaven is to be asked also to stay the night after. You'd imagine that your hosts would have had quite enough of everyone after the last drive and the offer of a quick cuppa, and would have planned to spend that evening quietly flaked out by themselves in front of the box with a couple of boiled eggs on the chest... But no: a dinner party has been organised, or even just a lovely cosy supper round a huge kitchen table, with candles guttering and the dogs' tails thumping by the Aga...What bliss.

Any weekend starts badly for me – I'm already exhausted from re-packing 38 times during the past five days – but shooting weekends in winter are the worst. Panic, trying to think of all the things I need – worrying again: boots need a boot-jack now; and not one but various jackets (for extremely wet, wet and not-so-wet); hats, gloves and mittens, waterproofs, silk thermals – all the kit. Oh, and the mantra, what was it ...? And then of course there's also all the extra staying-for-the-night-Friday-*and*-black-tie-Saturday gear. Then the three-hour drive – five if it's West Country – on Friday evening in the rush hour/gales/thick fog... Arrive too early as usual (train fever, impossible to cure) – 6.05 rather than 7pm as bidden. Have to spend intervening fifty-five mins parked 500 yards off from main gate in pitch dark and with lights off, praying not to be accosted for vagrancy. Or raped. (If raped, no point screaming, no-one'll hear. If accosted, have now got guns in the back, so will also be had up for Loitering With Intent. And have left solicitor's number in book at home so will be locked up in police station and no-one will ever know...)

Finally am so cold and jangling with Terror of Unknown (Rescue Remedy and Dr. Bach's Mimulus hidden in back under luggage, in first aid box already bulging with knife/corkscrew, bandages, metal file, hammer, brandy and enough kit for major brain surgery – talk about 'Be Prepared') and desperate need to pee, so give in and drive up to house, practising excuses for gross social ineptitude of arriving too early.

They talk of 'hosting a shoot'. Which of course is right: it's the man who usually deals with everything in the sporting department. But doing the 'hostess' part of a shooting party is damned hard work, and more so if you're going to make each guest feel special, which is the whole art of the thing. A girl-friend of mine, whose husband runs a shoot, is so good at it she should actually be giving courses on 'How To Be The Perfect Shooting Wife'. ('Shooting Wives' sounds more like a themed weekend actually: firearms provided, cheaper than a divorce.)

You arrive at their house (as per para. 2) too early and feeling therefore guilty as well as frozen to the marrow. But the automatic lights go on over the front door as you drive up, and as you open the driver's door and fall out thankfully onto the crunchy gravel you can hear heels clattering inside and shouts of joy. And she comes hurtling out, arms wide, burbling 'Thank GOD you've come darling we've been ACHING to open the bubbly come straight in loo's second on the left don't THINK about luggage John'll take your gun and things watch the step you must be exhausted...'

The warm welcoming house smells of hyacinths and Czech & Speake candles. There are pristine unwrapped soaps, fresh Floris oils and new rolls of loo paper in your bathroom. In your bedroom, together with lots of lights, there are flowers on the dressing-table, little baskets of goodies and cotton-wool, and a pile of new books. And a spare adaptor in case you need it for your curling tongs; and a hair-dryer; and the comforting sight of flexes leading from the bed which assures you of a heated bed later on... Other guests arrive, dinner is perfect, the house rings with talk and laughter.

Next morning, breakfast (all the papers laid out, and about a dozen dishes) is gargantuan and delicious. Your wellies have been removed from your car, re-washed (you always wash your boots before going to a shoot, but here they don't take anything for granted) and laid out in the line of other boots by the gunroom door. The other guests and guns are, like the host, merry and relaxed and there's lots of cheerful banter. The shoot is brilliant: like the household, everything goes like clockwork and gives the illusion of being totally effortless; long drives of magical high partridges and tall gliding pheasants appearing (apparently) from nowhere, no sign of beaters harrying crops, shouting or cursing their dogs. Elevenses appear: forget the old bits of pre-wrapped B.R. cake tasting of terminal hyena, the 'here's-something-we-made-last-year' paralysing potcheen. It's hot bull-shot and honey-smothered sausages and sweet muffins and The King's Ginger.

Lunch is in the heated village hall: bubbling dishes and parsnip puree and yummy pud. (with *clotted* cream) and Paxton's cheeses and warm crusty bread and beer and elderflower and claret. Back at the house for tea: thinly-sliced cucumber sand-wiches like your grandmother had, and cake, by a roaring fire – do you *wonder* that I go on about food? – and then a bath and a long, delicious nap in warmed embroidered sheets. Dinner is sumptuous, noisy and funny; and you stagger up the stairs well past midnight thinking this is exactly what heaven must be like,

being cosseted and spoiled beyond even your wildest dreams. And as you leave the next morning, they're still saying WHY do you have to go, why not stay the week and, incredibly, sounding as if they really meant it.

But even had it not been so utterly perfect it would still have been wonderful of course: a day and a stay with friends, gorgeous countryside, good sport and, above all, the matchless camaraderie of a shooting party. And there isn't a single host, or a hostess, in the land who doesn't work their socks off trying to make sure their guests are happy. It's usually the guests who create the most problems. Latterly I was told of an unforgiveable and, sadly, English, couple who – obviously under the arrogant misapprehension that they were not going to be as 'properly' looked after as they clearly felt was their due – turned up for a partridge shoot in Spain (three days' shooting, staying in a lovely house with charming Spanish hosts), bringing with them – it's unbelievable but I swear it's true – their own food, their own wine, *and their own candlesticks...*

Had I been the hostess, I'd have known exactly what to do with the candlesticks.

Writer's Block

Every so often the muse fails, inspiration grinds to a halt, the screen remains a *tabula rasa* and you know for certain that the time has finally come to hang up the mouse. I find that in my case it occurs quite regularly – about once a month around deadline day actually; but then, with a lot of luck and after much supplication for divine intervention, something usually clicks to 'On' and you can just about wing it. Not always, mind you; but it is at such times however – when what is laughingly known as the mind has gone AWOL and the dark night of the soul kicks in – that a totally unprofessional scribbler such as myself is, as they say in some quarters, so very, very blessed. In moments of stress, we 'contributors' have our very own Samaritan to hand, the Editor-in-Chief, a veritable star amongst men, who, in his inimitably kind, patient and serene way, holds your hand over the e-mail, dispenses inter-galactic Kleenex and sage counselling and seam-lessly smoothes everything out. I can think of no more tedious a

job than having to deal with a hack whose creative process is out to lunch. But then probably neither can he.

There don't seem to be any rules as such about 'contributing'. Personally, and happily, I don't have to write about specifics so my own criterion is, simply, no names, no pack drill. *Ever.* Once you start identifying places or shoots by name, however complimentary you may be about them, you're toast. It's simply Not Done. A social no-no, rather like borrowing cash off the head keeper for the bar bill.

Last year I had gorgeous invitation to an early day at the partridges, which turned out to be (as I lay, remembering every bird, later on in the bath) probably the very nicest shooting day of my life. Although a very good and truly 'wild' pheasant shoot, on which it is 'cocks only' as a matter of course, this estate had not shown partridges before and, having warned all his guests well in advance, our host was fairly fatalistic about what we might see on this first-ever 'experimental' attempt. In the event, it was the greatest possible success. The weather was perfect – blue skies and a good wind. The place itself is a dream, lovely old parkland with huge and beautiful trees and a plethora of wild life; pheasants scurried about, and took off in that irritatingly loud and *vulgar* manner that they usually affect only when they know that either they're out of season, or it's Sunday; roe rushed through the line, hares sat up and twitched black-tipped ears before lolloping on, and a skein of geese came over in the first drive, which (naturally) we all turned to watch at precisely the moment that the first of the coveys came bombing out...

It was a lovely relaxed party, the keepers were charming and extremely smart and highly efficient with their immaculately-behaved dogs; the beaters were out in hordes, smiley and garrulous before we all set off, or between drives but – most remarkably – totally silent in the beating lines. And there were partridges, high and fast, a-plenty. The only problem was that we were all so pleased to be there, and with such good friends, and kept enjoying and admiring, quite loudly, everything so much, that we did rather fail to concentrate properly on the job in hand, and subsequently did not do sufficient justice either to the birds, or to the host's and the estate's, previous months of very hard work. Added to which the birds, who had obviously never done this sort of thing before and who hadn't (to be fair) seen a copy of the script, were as wild as hawks and amazingly blasé, and left us all feeling rather foolish.

Having already given us, and the beaters and keepers, copious elevenses – cold slivers of roe fillet, an amazing array of schnapps and gins and other goodies, and the best hare soup ever – our darling hostess then produced a fantastic luncheon in the big old barn where (again, together with every single one of the keepers and the beaters – an unusual and fun and totally idiosyncratic way of looking after *everybody* really properly on a shooting day) we were all a noisy group of 30-odd people, all talking nineteen to the dozen and being wined and fed like kings...

The drive after lunch was a triumph, with high birds bursting out over tall trees causing much general excitement amongst the guns; and then to the last drive, where a long line of flag-bearing beaters appeared, descending slowly and silently down a hill and up the valley towards the guns, as ancient and somehow as regal a sight as if you were watch-ing a mediaeval Tainchel taking place... No-one counted cartridges, no-one minded how you shot, you were among good friends both old and new in this most

beautiful place with the most generous and marvellous hosts. And, to cap it all, your gun was cleaned for you before you left... It just couldn't have been a more perfect day. And I won't, of course, divulge where it was.

A thought: If, however, you do ever mention a location by name, it is of course vital to get that name right... To my good friend Malcolm Innes, a mine of Scottish anecdotes and informa-tion, I owe the following: Overheard in Edinburgh: two old Morningside biddies discussing an on-going and much-hyped legal trial, with especial attention to the prostitute who had allegedly been involved in the case. *'Wail'* says one, *'Ai* hurrd that she came frae Sco'land – one of the ailands in fect – Tiree was it now?' 'Och fer God's sake Morag,' sniffed the other, 'wha' aiver will you say next? Of *coorse* it wasna' Tiree – she was a Coll gurrul.'

Diary of a London Girl
(with apologies to B. Jones)

October 26th.

Panic stations. Woken this morning by telephone call at sparrow's by so-far-unimpressed guy who's never really spoken to me properly before. Bad timing, as actually wasn't really compos i.e. totally dysfunctional after fairly heavy session last night with girl-friends and Chardonnay. Anyway he made polite noises then asked me to spend next Saturday with him 'on a shoot in Hampshire'. Just like that. Totally stunned by this very fast move, all I could think of was to ask which film was it for? Long silence. Finally: 'I say, you are a scream' – obviously thought I was just being extremely witty. He then went on to explain what (as he put it) 'was entailed' and 'what fun it would be'. Hmmm... think he's chosen wrong playmate here as don't know first thing about outdoorsy things especially not shooting birds which sounds weird and obviously requires energetic participation even from spectators, not a Good Thing when consider that only exercise taken in last 24 months has been shopping... Anyway urgently needed to get back to sleep so said yes which now realise was terrible mistake but can't call and cancel as he'll think (rightly) that am wimp of first order. And although scary he's really dishy Colin-Firth-Lookalike. Sheer enormity of prospect going to demand huge amount of Dutch courage so after first caffeine intake rushed out to shops for bulk-buy of chocolate to alleviate terrors of anticipation.

Midday. O God, it'll be unmitigated disaster, C-F-L will sneer at my pathetic attempts at sophistication and will leave me behind tree in wilds of countryside, make me feel like idiot, no-one will talk to me all day and I'll be fatter than everyone else. Whythehelldidlagree. Damn and blast early-morning surprises. Chocolate was good idea though. Better go and buy shooting magazine to mug up on terminology and see what sex-goddess should wear in country.

Afternoon. Crikey. Just returned from local newsagents where was greeted with Shock-Horror: 'WHAT sort of magazine?' Then lots of teeth-sucking and po-faces and 'O no dear, we don't stock things like THAT here'. Might as well have been asking for *S.M. Monthly.* (Come to think of it when you see what IS stocked on the top shelf, makes you wonder whether shooting birds is really worse.) As admittedly recent but now pig-headed enthusiast, then had heated argument with f***wit salesgirl as to why, if city residents are allowed guns to shoot things with, they're not allowed to read about using them? Had to leave in hurry, they were about to ring for reinforcements.

Rang Rosie for help and advice as she has boyfriend who totes; said not to panic and she'll lend me gear, green wellies and ear-muff-things which apparently are required accessories, and then dropped by with copies of various shooting mags. for 'in-field fashion' she said. Gosh people in field look fearful, like have been kitted out in charity shop. Obviously not *haute couture* scenario here which is big relief as can do charity shop look. Ate most of chocolate whilst trying to decide which instant diet would best work so could squeeze into ex's old gardening trousers. Can hide un-do-uppable waistband with most fave. big brown polo-neck if necessary, though might have to coax three-year-old bathroom paint off bosom area (white-with-hint-of-lilac – probably not generally acceptable as shooting colour). Must remember to re-do roots as country looks windy in all photos. Intake of fags up 98% and now need more chocolate.

November 2nd.

Tomorrow looms... Dear God let me suddenly have appendicitis or something terminal as credible excuse for cancelling. Feel really yuck as stayed up all last night washing/tinting hair, de-foliating all obvious body-parts, drinking up ends of things, trying on clothes, practising make-up for outdoor life (blue eye-shadow too obvious so prob. best none), smoking 487 cigarettes, panicking and ringing my mother who wasn't any help at all. 'How thrilling darling, what FUN, now just relax and enjoy it, and remember that there's a First Time for Everything...' – oh purleese... Rosie though has been star, wrote out list of instructions like Don't talk during drives (luckily going in his car and it'll only take 90 mins. so can always pretend I'm asleep) and Don't scream when gun goes off and Don't say ah poor thing if shot bird goes hobbling into bush and Don't drink anything out of a flask (eh?) oh and apparently picking-up is legit. country occupation (glad she mentioned that) and mobile phones are not and Don't wear tights with holes as you have to take wellies off for lunch. Also lent me horrid waterproofy jacket to go over sweater and hide remaining immoveable hint-of-lilac splodges. Jacket smells of sick but she said it was spaniel and that all proper old Barbours smelled like that. (Thought proper old barbers smelled of carnation hair tonic actually but didn't argue.) Weather-forecast deeply worrying: how many vests can I stuff on without looking like Michelin ad? Why is dress-code for country so turgid? If I wear thick woolly longjohns will trousers even make it up above knees? Why did I agree to this anyway?

November 4th.
Survived yesterday – whew. No rain so didn't end up looking like wet cat and trousers made it and C-F-L really sweet and not scary at all. Think I managed ok (not gabbling on too much etc. or drinking anything AT ALL in case became totally insensible and fell over) and didn't make total horlicks except when asked to fetch large dead bird lying on ground and I did and he said (nicely though) Not like that, you always pick a bird up by the head, which was gross. Everyone v. friendly and helpful, some sweet old codger asked if it was my first time, which was funny. C-F-L talked non-stop all the time AND during both drives esp. the one coming home so Rosie wrong about that, and we stopped for long cosy booze in pub on way back. Then dropped me home and gave me dead bird he'd brought back and asked me to movies next week which bodes well. Rang Rosie later to ask what to do with bird and tell her I'd followed all instructions to letter and that some big Labrador peed in one of her wellies during lunch.

Fine Fare

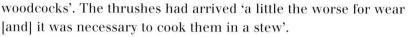

In November 1633, Galileo's daughter Suor Maria Celeste writes from her convent outside Florence to thank her father for the pannier full of game birds that he had sent by messenger. This included 13 thrushes and some 'grey partridges and woodcocks'. The thrushes had arrived 'a little the worse for wear [and] it was necessary to cook them in a stew'.

You can just imagine the scene: fearful excitement at the arrival of the tantalising cloth-covered pannier, only to find it full of small and decidedly well-past-sell-by-date decomposing corpses, each of which requires plucking, cleaning and, somehow, dealing with. And it is therefore at this point that one of the lowlier novice Sisters is summoned and detailed off to kitchen duty without more ado while Mother Superior, entertaining the scion of the local nobility in anticipation of his customary generosity to the community, plays with her rings and her beads and her fine glass of wine as her important guest languidly anticipates the forthcoming feast...

Fast-forward a few centuries and change the venue and we're on familiar ground here, we novices of the sporting life, we patient women, we faithful tenderers of home and hearth. It is evening, and raining, and November, and after the day's storms the countryside is quiet save for the two resident little owls ('Mills' and 'Boon'), who sit in nearby trees calling anxiously to each other across the dark... But hark my lady, be they not brakes squealing in yonder courtyard? Indeed, and followed by much banging of doors and swearing and what seems to be an unnecessary amount of parade-ground invective along the lines of 'cummere ya bugger, guwan, geddin there, arghh, no, not you, bloody idiot, leaveit damn you' etc. The Master and His Dogs are home from the hill, all of them sodden and covered in mud and filth and briars and feathers and blood. And he, never stopping even to remove his boots ('just like Marlborough', she whispers, her heart a-flutter – so great must surely be the impatience of his manly desire), squelches like a wet Yeti through the hall shouting for attention – 'Oy, fish-face, where are you, we're back' – before stomping into the kitchen and chucking handfuls of unrecognisable things with beaks and feet on into the sink with a peremptory 'there you go', while the dogs bark madly for their food and rush through unnoticed and unchecked into the drawing room to dry themselves off on the rare and important rugs scattered about the fine carpet...

After this he expects fulsome praise, the aforementioned boots pulled off for him and a large whisky and a hot collation ready by the fire. 'That's the ticket. Oh and give the dogs a towel down before you run my bath will you old thing?' Brilliant. The romance of sport.

Not for nothing are women credited with a superior mental agility, a greater courage, a more delicate and sharper perspicacity and a higher echelon of generosity, self-sacrifice and devotion than their male counterparts; and nowhere is this more instantly self-evident than in the culinary department. After the initial stomach-churning revulsion, the genes kick in – imagination, unflappable competence and guile. Just as their sisters in the Florentine convent, from time immemorial women have learnt to cope with the unspeakable and produce the eatable – nay, even the gastronomic delight. First of all there was, of course, the wretched numble pie. Then the stew – that most ubiquitous and possibly cleverest of disguises, which for generations has successfully and brilliantly hidden many a horror with impunity. Later still – a further and more sophisticated refinement – the game pie appeared for the *fêtes champêtres*, a cunning and aesthetically more palatable offering wrapped in heavily-decorated pastry, which could thus incorporate with even greater subtlety not only the hunter's triumphant offering but God knows what else besides – safer really not to enquire – and guaranteed to outwit even the most discerning male taste buds...

I have to tell you too that there are also, even in the less sophisticated parts of the world, native women who are no strangers to this sort of cunning cuisine. (Even in the so-called sophisticated parts, come to think of it: Isherwood was once given lung soup in Berlin.) Go to parts of India or Africa, to desert tribes or the denizens of the frozen north, to Uzbekistan or Ulan Bator, Turkmenistan or Tibet, and you will find the local women hard at work, transmogrifying the more repellent bits of local dead, frequently decomposing and fly-blown, fauna and other *trouvailles* (yak or armadillo, badger entrails and horse, rat, monkey or cat, wasps' nests or puffin, hyena and lizard, inner tyres or minced fur, bear, toad or goat – and once, never to be forgotten, a human finger nail) into fine dishes for local feasts and for their men's delectation. Baldrick should have been a woman. And, as has always been traditional amongst women everywhere and through the ages, to make it even more delightful a repast, this *quid pro quo*, this pound of flesh, this gastronomic revenge is delivered invariably with self-effacing modesty and with the sweetest of smiles...

No surprise therefore that we women out on shooting lunches usually stick to cheese and apple and the odd bit of fruitcake and generously leave the main offering for those unwitting, ravenous, wonderful men. We've all of us had our own moments of wily triumph. We *know*. Do you wonder that it was a woman who invented haggis? It must have been such a sweet revenge. 'So, Wully, whaur's yer *salade tiède de ris de veau au coulis de framboise fraîche* the noo?'

Weather to Shoot...?

ey ho, the wind and the rain... It's so much nicer going out
to shoot when it's warm and sunny (not too sunny of
course, birds don't like it), with a few white clouds scud-
ding across an azure heaven, a good brisk wind, and the autumn
colours glowing like jewels against the still-green countryside...
Occasionally it's also fun to shoot, not *when* it's snowing, as you
get disconcertingly blinded by snowflakes, but *in* the snow
(although birds don't like that, either: makes them all disorientat-
ed as they can't tell where the ground is. Apparently); but that's
only fun because it gives the female participants a chance to wear
fur and look exotic. Though when it's so cold you can't feel your
fingers any more, then it's definitely not fun; and standing in that
funny attitude of legs crossed whilst fumbling to warm hand in
crotch is never, it has to be said, the most alluring of positions for
a lady.

Talking of cold, it must be something to do with genes, or fat
or trust deposits, but men don't seem to feel the cold. As far as I'm
concerned, being warm is one of life's absolute priorities, but then
attention to personal comfort isn't really a manly attribute, especially in the older rather more serious generation who appear to
equate hardiness with godliness. That wonderful invitation to stay
('oh and black tie for dinner, can you bear it, George always
insists, so sorry') at the huge old shooting lodge on some storm-
lashed northern promontory, and your heart plummets as you
arrive in the teeth of a gale in the dark echoing sub-zero hall with
dead glassy-eyed decaying stags' heads looming down over the
stone flags where the hostess is wearing mittens to greet you and
you *know* there isn't the remotest chance of there being even a
bulb within reach to warm your hands on let alone an actual
heater, and the plugs are early-1920s two-pin so you can't even
switch your hairdryer on to full blast to frighten the draught from
under the bedroom door, and there'll be that long, gut-chattering
gallop along to the Siberian bathroom with its permafrost lino
flooring... Call me picky, but I've never understood why it is so

much nobler in the mind to climb between freezing sheets in an arctic room in which the icicles form *inside* the windows...

'We're a very hardy lot up here y'know' cries your host, clad in Nanny's old cardigan and two puffas under his smoking jacket. The food at dinner bears the unmistakeable chill and hue of death, although the lovely old wine is bubbling, having been dumped and forgotten several hours ago in a pan on the Aga – had it been *chambré'd* it would have perished anyway. Even the dogs are thin and whimpering and hogging the fumes from the lone wet log, and all you want to do is break up every scrap of the (probably priceless) furniture and throw it into the magnificent stone fireplace with its armorial bearings and scream something Dante-esque before thankfully leaping in to the bliss of roaring flames... You can't even sit up all night drinking neat whisky to stave off hyperthermia as it doesn't, and anyway you've got to be able to see straight to shoot tomorrow. 'Ready for bedfordshire then? You won't be wanting anything silly like a hotwaterbottle now will you...' It's a statement, not a question, and you don't argue. I once spent the whole of one January night wearing every bit of clothing I possessed under the single blanket, weeping with the cold. Next morning, over the bleeding kidneys: 'Sleep well did you? Good girl, that's the ticket.'

I know: this has nothing to do with the weather as such, but it's symptomatic of general English *sang froid* (and I'll bet that was never a phrase coined by chance). Where were we... yes,

climate: so we are now left therefore with the most usual and, given the global positioning of these islands, prevalent weather in which we have to shoot most of the time, namely the rain. And birds (especially the human ones) hate rain most of all.

It's not the waterproof get-up, which does nothing for the image but you've got to look professional so it's just about bearable; it's the wet-hair bit which gets to us females really. Ok in sun-drenched St. Kitts, not ok in sodden St. Mellion. And then trying to dry it off for lunch under the hot-air hand-drier in the pub loo. (However brilliant your wet-weather gear, the hat is never quite good enough is it? And no lady would be seen shooting, or indeed dead, in a cagoule. The motor-bike helmet apart, proper totally-non-permeable headgear for girls has still to be invented.) That, and the general unattractiveness of humanity out in the field makes a misery of those wild, horizontal-rain-lashed, miserable winter days when everyone has 'flu and people hack and spit and snuffle, sneezing out germs and sporting nose-drips and being totally incomprehensible as they mumble their way round foul-smelling cough-sweets built for seamen in the Antarctic.

(Judge to Counsel: 'Mr. Smith, your client seems to be much incommoded by his cough. Get him to suck a Fisherman's Friend, or something of that ilk.' Counsel: 'Thank you, my lord; but my client' *[on charge of indecent assault in public lavatory]* 'is in quite enough trouble as it is...')

Before shooting anywhere in winter, I spend several days glued to the weatherman on the box, or the five-day forecast on the internet, so as to have some sort of inkling of what's in store. Not that it makes any difference of course, but it's easier to *know*. At least it does mean I'll have all the right equipment, and will have already put in the lenses so as not to have to suffer the humiliation of fumbling about under a bush trying to get the damned things in the right way round or having to shoot in a downpour with specs on. (Laser treatment, that's the answer.) Your hosts aren't terribly helpful if you ring them prior to setting off either. 'Yawhat?... erm... don't know, mist's still down. Have a word with the old bag, more in her line of country, hmm? Whad'you mean, bring a brolly..? oh right... ha ha ha' and you can just see him slamming down the phone and muttering 'silly cow' into the toast and marmalade and making a mental note to put you out on the end in the bare

field when they're doing that big wood before lunch so you'll get soaked good and proper – ' teach her'.

One evening, I unthinkingly rang my next day's host, knowing that storms were meant to be 'moving through'- simply to find out whether they'd got to his area yet. 'Storm? No idea. Wait one, I'll ring the Met.' 'No no, for heaven's sake don't go to all th... I mean, what's it doing outside the window?' 'Can't see. Mrs. Thingummy's drawn the curtains.' Oh boy. Two points higher on his IQ and he'd have been a rock.

Fog is only a real problem if you're the host of course, when it's a nightmare. I once arrived, invited as a 'fill-in', at a fog-bound corporate day where the clients, mostly European, had flown in especially and the shoot-manager didn't have the gumption to cancel the first drive, or even delay it an hour or so whilst praying for the stuff to clear. We lined out obediently therefore with loaders, pickers-up and all, faced with a white-out like a concrete wall approximately ten yards ahead of the line. The drive started, there were muffled cries from lost beaters within but, unsurprisingly, nothing emerged. After 45 long minutes of zilch, the fog began to rise. About six inches. It was just enough (we were finally beginning to make out the surreal ghost-shapes of beaters slowly looming forward) for us all suddenly to notice that, under the white curtain ahead, a dark mass of something was moving silently over the ground towards us.

What must have been the entire county's population of game-birds, having gallantly made it on foot below the fog, now stood shuffling together, peering out in a puzzled fashion at the clear daylight and the guns in front of them, before scurrying quietly on through the line. No-one moved, or uttered, until they were safely through.

Moments to Avoid

———◆———

I hate all these modern machines that TALK to you. I have a microwave that questions every mortal thing I do with it. 'Have you weighed the meat?' it asks querulously; 'have you washed your hands before handling it?' Next it'll be 'Do you know that the meat you are cooking is beef and you will soon go mad?' or 'Are you having a bad hair day?' Talk about the nanny state. I once had a car that did it too: 'You have forgotten to apply the brake' it sneered (*after* I'd hit the car in front. Who the hell did it think it was – Mystic Meg?). 'You are low on petrol' it would suggest smugly, as I drove off. THAT'S WHY I'M GOING TO THE GARAGE YOU STUPID BERK. No wonder people suffer from road rage.

Mind you, it's not that one couldn't do with a bit of help from the car now and then – a gentle reminder on the lines of '*Don't shut the door the keys are... oh well, bad luck.*' And on shooting days, an in-flight check-list could be handy. 'Gun?' 'Roger'. 'Earmuffs?' 'Roger'. 'Waterproof mascara?' 'Wait one...' It's no joke: I forgot that one once, and we were trying to remain vertical in the teeth of driving sheet-rain for the whole day. Walking up to the guests' transport vehicle at the end, I happened to glance (as one does) into the side-mirror and caught sight of this terrible panda face, wearing my hat... Bit of luck I checked. The well-organised woman has her eyelashes dyed – and/or the eye-liner tattoed on, it works a treat – *before* the shooting season opens.

I have to confess that,

although it's wondrous being a woman and I wouldn't swop for anything, there are the occasional downsides. A shooting lunch 'back at the house', you've just got half-drowned in a tempest, and you're there in the cloakroom desperately trying to dry your hair off with loo-paper so as not to muss up the hostess' smart little monogrammed linen guest-towels, and then have to spend the ensuing hour looking like Rapunzel with attitude. Or out stalking, and finally you just HAVE to find a bush which, as in Reed's *Lessons of War*, 'in your case you have not got'; while out there somewhere, glued to his binoculars, the pony-boy is watching you flashing your surrealistic semaphore across the darkening hills...

How did they do it, those intrepid female travellers in days of yore, coping with fevers and prickly heat and *consaca* and bloody flux, beset by plagues and scorpions and bandits and millipedes in the bedding, fording rapids, staggering across the burning savan-

nah and through steaming jungles? Any man will counter this by explaining that it was all done by 'not worrying about the mascara, that's how, my girl. Wouldn't catch Karen Blixen messing about with the war-paint before going off to shoot lions. Dammitall, a woman should have her priorities and her hormones straight if she's going to join the gentlemen's world, what?' *Right*; so no HRT in the howdah then...

Rubbish. This is a purely British, male, point of view. Jane Digby put on silken robes and all the *khol* she could muster before following her beloved Midjuel into Palmyra; and any halfway decent British mem'sahib would have known how to quell a riot and stop a tiger in its tracks too, with or without the *papier poudré*. Women are still – understandably – expected to be just as competent now, but the men don't have time for niceties. 'No NO you stupid woman, it landed over there, in the thorn hedge, now for God's sake just GET IN THERE and GET the bloody thing and stop worrying about your damned nail-varnish...' Fair enough I suppose: you're not there for decorative purposes after all. But it's the old dilemma, coping with the double standards: a lady in the shooting field is expected to be a lady (so no two-fingered gestures from behind the line, or you'll be sent home) and yet be as 'tough' and as game and as sporting as the fellers and cope with everything the way they jolly well do, by Jove.

I spent the most miserable day of my shooting career late last year at one of those really famous, prestigious shoots down in the West Country, the sort that are so superb and fantasmogorical that grown men actually blub if they find they have been left off the invitation list. I was anyway stunned to be asked – I mean I simply do *not* shoot well enough to contribute my share of the bag on those sorts of days. (Actually I always reckon I only get asked if the host needs to keep the numbers down for PR purposes on what otherwise could have been a day on which they *might* have been deemed to have 'rather overdone it'...) Anyway there I was, game and grateful and part of the line, standing deep in a combe in weather that normally I would cheerfully eat my own arm rather than have to go out in. Fair-weather shot? That's me, petal: 'Give me sunshine' is my signature tune...

The forecast had been frightful – 'severe gales gusting up to 98mph.' and all that spiel, with radio warnings to stay indoors for fear of being killed by flying rooves or cattle or falling asteroids. The storm had started at midnight, and both wind and rain were so strong that, at breakfast earlier, the hostess' cat had come hurtling through the cat-flap with all four paws in the air in front of it and landed straight inside the fridge opposite, the door of which by pure chance happened to be open. The first drive was just horrendous. The birds were in outer space and obviously on speed and as well every thermal going, and I could make no sense of them whatsoever.

It didn't get any better either. That evening at dinner, I asked my neighbour what one did when the wheels had fallen off all day. Mostly to be polite and make conversation, you understand, as he was one of those smug fraffly-fraffly types whom you long to see skid straight into the soup. He purred almost audibly at the sheer *naivete* of the question. 'But my *deah* lady' (don't you just want to GAROTTE any man who talks down at you in that superior, wooden-top fashion; he couldn't say his r's either which made it worse) 'my *deah* lady, surely they don't ever come orf ALL DAY... a single dwive perhaps, but then you shuwly just work out what you're doing wong, and put it wight.' He smiled pityingly and turned away. The really irritating part was that I knew that he was, of course, absolutely correct.

What I was not going to mention to him, or anyone else for that matter, was that I knew exactly why I'd shot even worse than normal all day. I'd broken a rib two days before – too late to renege – and was strapped up like a mummy on painkillers. But to have confessed to it would have been considered wet, 'girly' and conduct definitely unbecoming an officer's daughter. I certainly felt guilty about my kind and unsuspecting host, but at least I had my female pride intact.

And I'd worn the waterpoof mascara that day, *and* it hadn't run. As a female in the shooting field, you have to hold on to little bonuses like that or you're done for.

Outward Bound

At a recent dinner party, my neighbour's rather startling opening gambit was 'So, d'you like hiking?' Well, no actually. Do I *look* like an Outward Bound girl? I was even thrown out of the Brownies for heaven's sake (never could do the knots). I don't hike, or trek, or do anything remotely survivalist like, say, the Yukon Quest – that ghastly 1000-mile race which includes four mountain ranges with nothing but a GPS if you're lucky and a team of huskies, and where the mercury can hit –60°C... Nor have I ever harboured the slightest desire to apply for a Delta Force badge or even, let's face it, to participate in that particularly English weekend-party torture of 'Ahh, a good brisk walk after lunch, right?' when all you want to do is curl up in front of the fire with a nice male / the Sunday papers. (Men have it much easier than women on weekend houseparties, have you noticed? They don't have to do things like having to change five times a day or make nice noises about the cook/recipes/garden/children/lack of heating. There's only *one* rule for men on houseparties which is 'Don't do the crossword, or the hostess, without asking first'. And some of them still need it explaining: semaphore's quite useful as older men on shooting parties tend, as we know, to be quite deaf.)

But *revenons à nos moutons*. Travel is one thing (after all, even the 18th century bluestocking ladies of the nobility did the Grand Tour, complete with servants, lovers and chaises); but trekking or hiking is, indubitably, quite *quite* different. Just take the clothes involved, for instance. I confess that, as a *travelling* lady, my ideal capsule wardrobe would consist of well-cut trousers, a large hat and lots of moisturiser, a couple of DKNY numbers, good footwear plus some strappy heels, Diamox in case of heights, a muff-pistol

and possibly a Brazilian waxer. It would absolutely *never* include crampons or a helmet of any kind, a fold-up kayak, a recipe for frozen walrus, or one of those dinky little 300K bergens that you just whip inside-out and it turns into a helicopter.

You can easily recognise hiking *aficionados*. Doesn't matter where it is – airport or train, city streets, dock-side or outer Mongolia – they're always surrounded by mounds of gear, focussed, intense, looking totally deranged and, thanks to the new *de rigeur* explorer-wear, 'endurance-tested both on Everest and beneath the Antarctic ice', all smelling like skunks. Once, on a plane to Kathmandu, where we were going *en route* to a fort-night's organised trip by coach across Tibet, I noticed that, regard-less of sex, everyone else's concept of in-flight fashion consisted of heavy boots worn with three pairs of socks and a vapour trail of unwashed extremities that would have choked a cat, lycra polo-neck T-shirts, BO you could have cut with a panga and swathes of jolly-coloured nylon ropes, belays and clips. Hikers, definitely. And that the daughter and I were the only people on the plane wearing both natural fibres *and earrings*. Call me superficial, but I don't see why you shouldn't make a bit of an effort, even in the remoter corners of the globe. And anyway, in the sort of places I like going, earrings usually work a treat as barter.

Hiking as such is, patently, *absolutely* not My Thing. However for some reason the prospect of slogging relent-lessly across remote, wild, pre-cipitous, unforgiving and hostile terrain in snow, lashing rain, white-outs and gales of 80 mph – and where the dangers of getting lost in fog, and of crevasses, rock-falls, brain-oedemas, instant demise and Air Rescue Teams with metal sleds are always distinct possibilities – is not only perfectly acceptable but, indeed, eagerly anticipated.

Why? Terminology, that's why: because it's not called 'hiking', it's called 'stalking in Scotland'.

We'd had a long, ghastly day after the hinds. It was December, and foul, but the cull had been scheduled to be completed that day. We'd laboured all over the hills, sheltering from storms whenever possible; we'd had three successful stalks and, finally, got the last of the beasts just as dark, and the fog, was closing in. 'Right mum' said the stalker after he'd called up the pony-boy on the radio to come out again for the final pick-up: 'Gimme the rifle, an' go up there onto that ridge bit where ye'll be out the wind; I'll go down and deal with the beasts, and I'll collect ye in about half an hour on the way back. Dinna budge though, as it'll be guy dark by then.' Fine. I struggled up onto the ridge, retrieved the last bit of chocolate out of my back-pack and snuggled down thankfully against the rocks to wait.

Two hours later, I was still waiting. (One of the cardinal rules of stalking is that you always do *exactly* as you're told.) The temperature had plummeted, the ice-ladened rain was horizontal and in the pitch dark the fog was now swirling about the ridge. I'd been checking my watch thanks to a lighter but that had now died. I was hoarse from yelling, but answer had come there none. Frozen and shaking, I'd been through the back-pack twenty times, but it still hadn't produced anything more useful than one heavy sweater which I was now wearing as a yashmak, some extra rounds of ammunition – useless without the rifle – assorted elastic bandages for sprains, a small box of fluff for checking light summer winds in gullies and an ancient Penguin biscuit. Brilliant. No flares; no compass; no emergency foil blanket or RT; no hailer, no fold-up microlite. *Nul points*. And, more irritatingly, if I subsequently expired from hypothermia, it would be entirely through my own stupid fault.

It later transpired that he'd trailed behind the pony-boy for the three miles or so back to the vehicles, and had helped unchain the beasts and got the horse-box hitched before the boy enquired blithely 'did he no' still have the lady with him?' At which point, it was reported, he 'struck the side o' the horse-box, an' uttered some powerful strong words' and set off back into the night...

Terminology be damned. Hiking in any shape or form can be hell.

A Politeness of Princes

Remnants of next-door neighbour's 18-year old's party spill out into street at 4.55am full of drink and shouts, with cars revving and squealing, and yelled dialogues, seemingly how all young communicate, while driving off. Had only managed to get to sleep an hour before anyway owing to thunderous woofer on their umpteen-squillion-decibel CD-player. My child was perfectly well-behaved, how come other people's so ill-mannered and LOUD? Long to hurl bricks/fulminations through open window, but it wouldn't look too good...

Plumber unexpectedly at front door at 7.30am interrupting sacrosanct newspaper/caffeine intake/quiet-moments-before-hurly-burly-of-day routine, full of baroque excuses as to why didn't turn up as arranged two months ago to fix leak, since when house has resembled that of early Irish bog dweller, littered with buckets and brown patches spreading like creeping lurgy. Why don't I live sensibly in a flat, where rising damp and bum roof-tiles are landlord's problem? Hate bloody roof with passion. Actually, hate mornings generally. Plumber requires polite but full attention, tea, ('two lumps fanks luv'), detailed tour and explanations. Explanations? Just look at water pouring down walls, for crying out loud. Apparently now need new asphalt, oh God. *And* am going to be late for City meeting.

All traffic at rush-hour standstill everywhere, natch, entailing lung-scorching sprint and indecently chaotic entrance into hallowed purlieus/board-room. Introductions all round for openers by inept but self-satisfied spokesman. '...and Mrs. S. who of course – er – well, who *shoots*, huhuh, and is eminently... etc. etc.' Silence. Understandable actually. Am in room filled with two dozen financial types whose idea of sport is probably derivatives, or whatever rhymes with banking; am here to discuss, at their suggestion, what sort of art should decorate their premises; am also only person present who is not male, chairman, foreign associate, board member, Square Mile whizz-kid, emperor or God. Despite earlier *débâcles* am turned out perfectly for Business In The City: briefcase, designer scarf, good suit, just enough leg, plain gold earrings – nothing sporty, no duck bottoms in sight, no road-kill fashion, nothing to frighten the horses. So why on *earth* the shooting reference?? Prat. Totally irrelevant. Actually, quite rude. What about mentioning impeccable art-world references / ab.fab.CV / other amazing talents?? Maybe am in wrong place? Maybe they need new spokesman?

After initial hiccup, all went fine. Was being seen out by nice chatty whizz-kid when one guy, who'd been sitting at far end of table, came up and introduced himself. 'Been hoping to catch a word with you – sorry about that really crass introduction. Do a bit of shooting myself, funny how some people react simply because you shoot occasionally...' I said thanks, not to worry, nothing terminal, you get used to it, and probably axe-murderers and nudists get same treatment. 'Tell you what, join me for a spot of lunch and I swear we won't mention it: how's about opera or archeology? Or your jewellery designing? Aha yes, got the spies out... And are you going to the antiques fair? Oh and by the way, just so's you know, liked what you wrote last month – where's your coat? Great, let's go...' What a prince.

After extremely boozy lunch, he returned to school and, lurching into taxi home, I got thinking about surreal experiences. Like when people I don't know from proverbial hole in wall sneeringly bring shooting into the conversation; and acquaintances who invariably ask 'So, been killing anything lately?' and always in those rather kind, *patient* tones as to someone severely mentally challenged who can't talk or think about anything else... Why? Are they actually interested (unlikely) or just being patronising (probably), talking 'down' as if one was very, very stupid... Anyway, shooting's not life-sentence like becoming Carmelite nun – well, not the way I do it. Hobby not vocation, dammit. And you don't enquire about someone's hobbies *every time* you see them ('so, what's new, how's the glue-sniffing / wife-beating / beetle-collection going?') – it's not polite, and there are umpteen more amusing subjects around... AND we were all taught early on that it is, after all, only good manners to put a modicum of effort into conversation. So this shooting-talk gambit is therefore simply laziness, and implies that they feel you're not really worth the extra effort... pigeon-holing, like at office Christmas parties; 'this is Joe Bloggs, he's in filing, this is Ribena Smith, she gives great hardcopies'... Uh-huh: mustn't get paranoid.

To do: Get CV up to date/printed out

        Practice death-stare to use on neighbour, will it achieve spontaneous combustion?

        Get more cartridges for next weekend.

Have to admit though that when total stranger comes up and confides that they've enjoyed reading something you've written – well, hey... And although they've probably mistaken me for A.N.Other, nevertheless realise that it could be embarrassing for them if they were made aware of their mistake, and so tactfully accept compliment with delight... *politesse* all round, everyone's happy. Convent education comes into its own, hooray...

Musing about good manners *et al*, remembered a story my father told me which had involved a brother officer of his, some-time in the late 1930s. Browsing the counters in Fortnum's, the officer saw a very pretty and obviously famous (lots of people clapping etc.) woman approaching through surging crowd. He *knew* that he recognised her, although he couldn't think exactly why, or where they'd met; but, undeterred, he approached, bowed very correctly and, greeting her with enthusiasm, proceeded to engage her in conversation – she was extremely charming – skirting round carefully to find a topic of conversation that might furnish him with some sort of clue as to why she was so familiar...

Finally, he hit on the perfect question. 'And your husband, these days... is... doing what?' She smiled up at him beatifically. 'Oh, still King' she replied, before gently and tactfully moving on...

Steady Under Fire

———◆———

T he telephone rang. It was just past seven in the morning. I'm not very *good* first thing (usually still asleep at that sort of time – 'town' you understand) and in fact would much rather not be spoken to by anyone until I've had the caffeine, put the face on and more or less got it all together. Getting up for a spot of roe stalking, or going out for the morning flight – now that's a different matter entirely; but early morning chit-chat, forget it. Especially when, after a couple of seconds, you realise it's the godfather, a dear old army friend of the parents, on the other end, deaf as a post and full of what Eeyore called *bonhommy*, so you really have to concentrate.

'H'ro? Uhhyesuhmm, s'Montyheahhhh, zatyooP'fahh?' Maybe it was a bad line, or did I have a hangover? But I said yes, it was, and went on with the 'Monty-goodness-how-lovely-to-hear-you' routine, trying to unravel sleep (the brain going like the clappers), and sound bright, bushy-tailed and half-way *compos*. 'Hmmm, meandahhCarline, wondahd'fyoud keahter comanstayanshoot 'na cuplamonthswhat... hmmm?... youstilltheah?' I said golly and how wonderful and thank you so much and when exactly and how was Caroline, and prayed I'd got at least the gist of it right. He waited a moment to make sure I'd finished talking – when you're that deaf you don't hear *words* on the other end of a line, just the sound of the other person's voice: when it stops, it's your turn again. 'Jollygoo'showo'thing' he bellowed, 'ahhh... whwhrumph AH YES, hmm, 'll sendyouaCARDhmmm?' and put the phone down.

He'd been in the regiment with my father ('m'half-section y'know') and was exactly the sort of Englishman that foreigners are terrified of meeting, mostly because they can't understand a word he says. He did also appear a trifle forbidding – tall and stentorian, goodly amount of weight, pale watery blue eyes, well-trimmed white moustache – but basically he was just a big old pussycat. He said things like 'well done' instead of 'thank you' when being helped over a fence out shooting – always denotes years of being nannied by a soldier-servant; never used 'paper tishoos' but kept a freshly-laundered handkerchief up his cuff, and complained loudly about any dish that wasn't 'decent joined-up meat'. He was however very partial to Marmite, especially on profiteroles – I got caught out on that one once – as they'd had it in the desert and 'it saved a lot of chaps' lives'.

They were all of an ilk, those retired brigadiers, colonels and generals, now well-on in years; some were Lord Lieuts., some, erstwhile members of the Upper House. They all lived peaceably in the country, had their early-morning tea at half past five and took the dogs for a walk on the dot of six-fifteen. They stood ram-rod-straight with wet eyes at the Service of Remembrance, doffed their hats to women, roared at their dogs and sons but were brilliant with small grandchildren. They remained improbably married either to small mouse-like wives who wore frilly-necked blouses and puffas for breakfast and never asked for the heating to be turned up but chirrupped 'isn't it a *lovely* day' whenever the sun shone; or to the sort of female who had probably been their driver during the war and was the living embodiment of that geophysical feature we all learned about at school, the Eroded Dyke, favouring sensible shoes and a Norwegian 'cardy' that looked as if someone had been sick over it and whose skin – a stranger to moisturisers – had clearly been exposed to nothing more nourishing over the past half-century than compost fumes.

What he was doing asking me to shoot I couldn't imagine (I mean, as a female you don't *get* asked to shoot by these old boys, any more than they'd ask you to share a cigar or put down one of their hunters) – probably quite simply because he was my godfather; so I'd just have to mind my eye when the day came as I knew he always invited his old cronies too and they were lethal.

He himself had gone on shooting until he was past eighty in spite, or perhaps because, of the fact that his wife Caroline (who was actually a very good egg indeed) had been trying for years to get him to stop. But then came a memorable morning up at the family place in Sutherland when the woodcock had been in and he and half a dozen old duffers were standing round some rhododendron bushes blasting away like it was Mersa Matruh all over again. Suddenly the keeper appeared, staggering out of the undergrowth in front of my godfather, clutching his face and bleeding profusely. 'I SAY Stewart, odearodearodear, youallrighth-mmm? mydearfeller, wouldn't've hurtyou foralltheworld...' 'Och dinna yous go frettin' about tha' General' came the laconic reply. 'Yer granfaither shot ma granfaither, an' yer faither shot ma faither, so it's only right you yerself should shoot me.' That shook him and, muttering something about 'not feeling quite the thing', he beat a retreat to the house and declined to shoot for the rest of the day.

In fact he never took his gun out again after that episode, much to everyone's secret relief. I always had a sneaking feeling that probably Caroline had given the keeper some ketchup and bribed him to do it.

He and Caroline lived in a wonderful time-warp of a house in Leicestershire, a lovely informal hotch-potch of a place awash

with baskets of terriers, old magazines and tatting, beautiful linen and faded chintzes and Edwardian letter-boxes and, in the hall, the most elegant little coaching-whip stand. Photographs of big-game hunts and old trophy heads hung in the cloakroom (white skulls of hartebeeste with ivory plaques inscribed 'Togoland 1910') and a stuffed stoat lived under the hand-basin. In the boot-room stood regiments of ancient highly-polished riding boots, for many years now unused, which were the pride and joy of a decrepit old family butler called Orchid – who had, he was always pleased to remind you, once loaded for a legendary shot in Aberdeenshire – who emerged every month out of some bolt-hole in order to buff them up together with the godfather's rows of leather shooting boots. 'Rubber boots? For the General? Indeed *not*, madam. The General only wears leather on his feet' he'd explained once when I'd asked.

Staying with the godfather for a shooting day, you had to have breakfast with your own obviously-polished, leather shooting boots *on*, as in true military fashion he would not tolerate any form of unpunctuality or being 'late for the orf'. Even an urgent call of nature was absolutely no excuse for tardiness, and I'd learned from Caroline that it was useless to plead. 'Haven't I just got time for a really quick dash upstairs Monty?' 'Certainly not. *Gentlemen*' (and this presumably meant ladies too) 'do such things *before* breakfast. Go before, or hang on till lunch.'

One Sunday in October when I was there, he read in the news-papers over breakfast that someone had died, leaving the whole of his very considerable sporting estate to a wildlife trust on con-dition that the property be demolished and the land used as a bird sanctuary. I thought he was going to have a seizure. 'Neverheardanythin' sobloodysilly 'nallm'life' he choked, toast crumbs exploding everywhere. 'Nambypamby sentimental-ity ofthewors'sort. Hopesome damnFOXgoesan' digshimup. Teach'im. Pansytoo, more'nlikely.' He took out his old pocket watch which was chiming erratically. 'Heavens is that the time... Cmo'now. Got your hat Caro? Can't be late for church and that sewerofavicar, silly arse. But, huahuahua, I've put in a Biddin' Prayer that'll sort him out, huahuahua.' We stood solemnly in the cold dark pews, listening to an urgent plea to the Almighty for a 'frost to get the leaves off the coverts, o Lord hear us'. The ensuing silence was broken only by the midge-like whine of his hearing aid and what sounded very like a snort of triumph.

Although by now he had given up shooting, he still enjoyed going out for the day to watch, so I asked him to accompany me and proffer moral support for what sounded as if it was going to be a fairly high-powered corporate shoot and one which I was dreading ('huh, southefenglandheh? quantity not quality, hmm?') with, according to the host, a number of 'important-business-wise' foreigners attending. The morning started badly, with a 'shoot manager' reading out the rules of engagement, which

included the injunction: 'Finally: a fifty-pound fine for a white pheasant. Oh, and a hundred for anyone caught using mobile phone, ha ha.' I couldn't believe my ears, and out of the corner of my eye, could see the hearing aid (which he only wore for shooting occasions) being turned up and a scowl crossing the face like a black cloud. 'WHAT did that feller say?' he enquired loudly, as we climbed into somebody's immoderately clean new Range Rover. 'Wha'wazzatallabout?... Mobilephones indeed – sounds like a spiv's convention. Mind you, bloody man, got up like a bookie's clerk, wha'canyouexpecthmmm?'

I managed to keep him away from some of the foreign participants who were eyeing him with some alarm, but he sat on his shooting stick behind me and was in fact remarkably well-behaved, grunting at some fairly erratic shooting by one of our neighbours in the line but grumbling only occasionally. He did manage to corner the 'manager' over lunch, who looked a trifle unnerved, but there was nothing I could do about it. Worrying about my companion did nothing to help the concentration, and apart from one or two birds which, as he commented kindly, had 'dashed themselves into the pattern', I knew I hadn't shot well.

At the end of the day, I drove us both home in companionable, easy silence. He dozed off in the car, then awoke suddenly, as if he'd just thought of something. 'Tell you what darling, got a bottle of the Boy waiting on ice, open that when we get home. Rough dayhmmm? Don'worry, you didn't do badly, considering. Can't'vebineasy with all that lot, and there's nothing wrong with your shooting manners – proud o' you. What'd they say in Lorne Campbell's citation, hmmm? "In all the glorious annals of the British army" ' (he was speaking very clearly now) ' "the conduct of this officer has seldom been equalled and never been surpassed". Tell you a thing though' and he started to chortle; 'that feller Skaigness or whateverhisnamewas – told me he'd had an'merican out last season who'd fired, you'll never believe this, fourhundred and seventeen cartridges and got one bird... make you feel any better hmm? huahuahua... fourhundredandseventeen cartridges... oh I'd love to have seen that... ohdear ohdearohdear...'

I felt as pleased as punch. Caroline said later that she'd never known him enjoy a day so much.

A Day in the Life of a Shooting Woman

8.15am After usual sleepless-with-anticipation night in lovely country house belonging to kind friends who've invited me to stay and shoot, breakfast, with all the stuff I never have at home i.e. porridge and crispy bacon and kedgeree and something else I can't quite make out (have put in long-range lenses as forecast says it's going to lash with rain later) but tastes like mouse droppings fried in patchouli. What? Ahhh, black pudding – right. Golly, will breeches cope all day? Feel like sumo wrestler.

8.53am. Panicky (third) flight round house for final check that gun is (a) in slip and (b) still *complete* – (know someone who actually forgot to take fore-end with him to a shoot) and that cartridges, gloves, ear-defenders, hat etc. etc. are actually still in host's car where I'd put them around 6.55am in case I'd forget them later. Then boots on and driven by host with other nice fellow-guests to meeting-place/pub five minutes away. Say howd'y-do to local guns and beaters and climb back into cars for transportation to first drive. Why am I doing this, I can't shoot for toffee. Have drawn 2 which is great as it's not, with luck, where the action's going to be. Just as well really – don't even touch a feather with the first seven shots and my neighbour's beginning to enjoy himself, irritatingly taking birds over my head. Just as I start looking for a deep hole to go and bury myself in, suddenly remember that I've forgotten to send a prayer up to St.Hubert before the drive. Situation improves. Drop a large black cock on my neighbour's dog just to make him mind.

Second drive ok, getting in the swing: some nice high fast partridges and a couple of devilish curling pheasants in v.strong wind. Rain not as bad as forecast and lenses not getting washed away, *D.G.* Break for mid-morning soup, then two more drives before lunch. Not doing too badly now, and the cartridge: bird ratio quite respectable. Bully for St. Hubert, praise be.

1.19pm. Back at the pub for lunch. As cars are parked five yards from main road, take gun in with me which causes much merriment (obviously I'm just a paranoid hysterical female); but have remembered to bring shoes for lunch, halleluja, which leaves certain other people looking sour as they haven't and wet socks on lino do nothing for macho image. Super lunch, plus masses of vino which I decline in case it sends me to sleep during afternoon drive. V.jolly lot of co-shooting guests, nothing frightening.

2.13pm. Having moved over to bar for coffee with somebody's girlfriend, was in midst of frightfully interesting confab about liposuction when we both suddenly notice that men have all left (must have missed the traditional 'three minutes to go gentlemen' bit). Panic stations, grab everything and hurtle out to car park where everyone's revving up and hooting horns and making jokey remarks about being kept waiting as usual by the females. No probs. though, convoy sets off at high speed down muddy lanes for final drive while I struggle into boots in back of car. Lots of 'this is going to be the big one, got enough cartridges have you?' and all that chat from host. Only wish I'd had time for swift visit to loo as rain has stopped and I could have removed lenses. Damn.

2.14.23pm. Penny suddenly drops. HORRORS. Managed to retrieve boots, but have only gone and *left the bloody gun in the pub haven't I...* oh mercy – *help...* Yelling 'STOP', begin to stammer out abject apologies – this has to be the most *unforgiveable* stupidity ever perpetrated... Sympathetic laughter from two other guns in car but host goes a deep and rather alarming claret colour and skids into ditch. Shoot-manager in vehicle behind screeches to untidy halt behind. Host and I leap out, me beside myself with shame and trying incoherently to apologise to all and sundry for such crass idiocy... Luckily, manager's very calm, gets on mobile phone and sends someone back to pub; 'and don't you worry about a thing, just stand on the road up by that gate and wait for him while I place the other guns down in the field there. He won't be more than five minutes – stop panicking, everything's fine'. Host, still scarlet with rage, doesn't utter but, whilst I go into overdrive, burbling on at him like some mad thing about how *awful*, how very *very* deeply and *truly* sorry I am, he hurls my cartridge bag out of boot, gets back into car, slams door and roars off up to

the gate, scattering turds of mud everywhere... Waiting alone by gate, watching other guns being led down into field below road – the most shaming, humiliating, awful moment of my life. Must be fully eight minutes before gun-bearer finally arrives back, and I gallop down like some lopsided camel, cartridge bag thumping about, still babbling dementedly, to join the line. 'Well done, don't worry, relax, stop fussing, you're not the first idiot to have done that' they all cry kindly... Mine host turns his back on me as I pass him going at speed.

This isn't the worst bit. The worst bit is that the beaters, out of sight though undoubtedly aware of events, have of course been in position for l5 minutes now, quietly tapping sticks high up behind the coverts and game crop on top of the next hill and waiting for the horn to sound; and the birds, having also waited patiently (they know the form) presumably get fed up, look at their watches and decide it's time to go anyway, signal or no signal. And they go. Away from the guns (natch) and yonder, running out from the farthest corner of the game crop and taking off in their hundreds – a long unending streamlined squadron like in one of those old war-films. Flagmen wave, small boys leap and shout, all to no avail. By the grace of God there are some birds left who haven't played follow-my-leader and whom the beaters finally manage to corral noisily and push out in the right direction. But the *very* worst of it is that – sod's law of course – most of them come straight over my peg and, what's more, I manage to shoot every *single* one... Host doesn't speak to me again that day.

Can't say I blame him actually. At least, and I know it for a certainty, that's one invitation I won't ever be getting again.

215

'Oh for a Man...'

———◆———

'Oh for a man, oh for a mansion in the sky', as the old Salvation Army hymn went. In the best of all possible worlds, and if it's her lucky day, a young lady need look no further than the shooting field to find her ideal man. Most shooting men are gentlemen. You cannot assume that all gentlemen will necessarily be good shots; nor can you assume that all men who shoot are inevitably gentlemen. But put it this way: if they *are* gentlemen, in the fullest sense of the word, and they also shoot, then, as a woman, you're absolutely quids in. For they will have all the qualities, the *desiderata*, you could possibly dream of. And their prowess on the shooting field will merely add to the long list of their many and multifarious accomplishments and qualities ('let me count the ways'). At his very best, at his zenith you might say, the gentleman shot is a veritable paragon of virtues, 'Omeyword yessah' as they say in the mess. He is indeed the true alpha male – what every woman wants in her list to Santa.

So who is this *nonpareil* amongst shooting men? He is of course talented, kind, charming and very intelligent, great SOH and so forth, and moreover has of course – so very desirable in both men and dogs as I'm sure you'd agree – beautiful manners. He would be both a consistently modest *and* an exceptional shot. A good gamesman, he also, somewhat unusually, reads prolifically, listens to music, loves art, films and the theatre; *and* probably waltzes like a dream, can quote Herrick and studies astrophysics as well. (A verray parfit knighte: notte serprisyngelie, methinken hee is ane Angell alreddye and wille pruve hymseve a farre farre bettair thinge nor ye Moriss dancynge ore ye peinte-dryeinge bloakes; soe gette ye skaytes onne whyle ye mayye...) He can also make a mean Bloody Mary *and* can fold a towel, albeit with a little help. He's brilliant with dogs, and only remonstrates with women if they try to carry their own suitcases. And when you are rabbitting on, as one does, about something marginally esoteric like for instance the Greek hendecasyllabic verse form known as *phalaecean*, he would know perfectly well that you were not referring, however obliquely, to any unattractive male disease. (I don't actually *know* anyone remotely like this, but it's your wish-list and I'm only suggesting all this rubbish as you might as well go for broke.)

There's only one real downside to any shooting man, however, and that is sex. A number of sports in this country – horse-racing, football, rugby, even cricket it seems – appear to be hotbeds, if you'll excuse the expression, of sex, drugs and violence. The single ray of comfort and sanity is shooting, which isn't. Never has been. (Well, not since Mayerling, which scooped top marks in all three categories, but that of course was in the 19th century, and abroad, so doesn't count.) This is simply because, despite the recent appearance of media and film personalities of all genders to be found in the modern shooting field, shooting is still basically run by gentlemen for gentlemen. And your average gentleman doesn't really spend too much time thinking about sex. It gets in the way of Really Important Issues like the dearth of decent cigars, or what's happening in the global markets or the Davos meetings or the grouse moors, or whether it was bought marmalade at breakfast which isn't officers' fare.

Added to which, gentlemen who shoot either do so five days a week during the season and are thus in a state of total decline come February and in need of a good holiday; or they work all hours in the City or the like, and bat furiously out of town every Friday evening in the rush-hour to Somewhere in the Country in order to shoot on Saturday, and are then far too tired and emotional even to think about any sort of bird that isn't fully-feathered. Either way, they haven't the time, or the energy, or indeed the inclination for any form of amorous or sexual dalliances during the shooting months, which are therefore what you might term a Close Season.

So the only way for a young lady actually to come in contact with this prime specimen is, of course, in the shooting field. However, the shooting field is the very last place on earth where any relationship between the sexes might possibly blossom. The gentleman will have his mind focussed solely on the serious business in hand, before, during and well after the day is out. Any attempt at seduction, vamping or even mild flirtation is therefore quite futile and, although a young lady may chirrup away charm-

ingly and to her heart's content – so long as it's only between drives of course – she will not receive, and should not expect, any
form of reciprocation from the object of her desire.

So forget sex or romance in the shooting field, and content
yourself with hope. It's a tough call. Even St. Hubert had to
renounce his life of wild excess, of hunting stags and chasing
women and drinking flagons of wine with his reprobate chums, in
order to become Bishop of Liege, as a result of which he was later
made patron saint of *La Chasse*.

As a lady desirous of a little help over delicate matters of a
sentimental nature, you could always try sending up a small
prayer to him; '*la chasse*' does, after all, embrace a multitude of
possibilities.

Alternatively, there is another little prayer which a girl-friend
sent me recently, which I have found to be generally rather effi-
cacious as it covers almost all eventualities, and is also extremely
useful before a day's shooting. It goes as follows:– *'Dear God, so
far I've done all right: I haven't lost my temper, I haven't been
greedy, grumpy, malicious, unpleasant, selfish or over-indulgent,
and I'm very thankful for that. But in a few minutes, God, I'm going
to get out of bed, and from then on, I'm probably going to need a
lot more help. Amen'*